GASTROPARESIS SUCKS!

Gastric Bypass Surgery Made it Better

GASTROPARESIS SUCKS!

Gastric Bypass Surgery Made it Better

One patient's struggles and journey to diagnosis and
self-discovery

By Jennifer Diaz

TABLE OF CONTENTS

Introduction

(Me at a few months old, 1978)

Hi, my name is Jennifer. I was born in 1978 to two 18-year-old teenagers and was raised by my grandmother. I was afraid of my parents, even though they weren't together. Unfortunately, in the home I was raised, we were taught not to speak up when we had issues or felt ill. The only person who I could talk to was my grandmother. She understood the best about what we were going through as children and allowed us to come to her without shutting us down. Because we were poor, we didn't really have a lot of food in the house. Due to the lack of food and not being able to eat three square meals per days as one should, I would constantly have stomach aches. Eventually, I couldn't take the pain anymore and brought it to the attention of my mother. She took it as complaining as she usually did whenever I tried to express myself about any problems I was having, so I learned to keep it quiet after.

(5- to 6-year-old me)

My struggle with food had already started here. We were poor and ate the food that was available.

This way of thinking creeped into my teenage years and affected my relationship with food. It also affected my body image. I hid myself under the pounds that kept creeping up on my tiny 5'1 frame. Since I was taught to keep quiet about what I was feeling, when I started having stomach issues, I didn't speak up. I thought to myself, "Who cares?" A s a teenager all you want to be is heard, especially when you have issues going on that you don't understand. The problem started out small. At first it was pain when I ate, then it was the bloating. The bloating wasn't too horrible, so I paid no attention to it. Eventually, I tried to reach out to anyone that would listen but no one did. I was scared and alone. Things stayed this way for a while.

Then adulthood hit, and just like many of us, I put my family's needs before mine and ignored the symptoms I was having. However, the symptoms started getting worse and were affecting my day to day. At this point, my symptoms were pain with eating, bloating, nausea, and feeling just blah, as if I was getting the flu. This was around 2009, after my then mother-in law and brother-in-law passed away. (Stress is a big factor in causing flare ups with Gastroparesis). I ignored everything I was feeling for a few more years after that.

In 2012, after having my gall bladder removed, my symptoms blew up and I decided to go to my doctor because I couldn't deal with what I was going through. At this point, I was having all the issues I mentioned earlier, on top of explosive diarrhea with everything I ate. It was smelly and I felt like something died inside of me from how bad the odor was. The referred me to a GI doctor who ran tests and couldn't give me a clear answer at this point, so I ran and didn't look back.

I started taking Imodium for the diarrhea and restricting food to see what was causing the problems. The problem, though, is that when you run away from a situation for too long, eventually it bites you in the butt. In 2014, I can remember having pain in my stomach every time I ate again, moments of having to run to the bathroom, and moments of constipation. Now, instead of having a faucet in my butthole, I felt like there was a plunger stuck and it wasn't letting anything out. At this point, I was pooping two times a week and it was painful. I felt like I had a baby coming out my butt. Since I was only pooping that little, I would get so bloated that I would look seven months pregnant and have strangers in the streets congratulate me on my pregnancy that didn't exist. I was honestly too embarrassed to correct them.

Trying to explain what I was feeling to people who weren't ill was frustrating. When I tried to explain my stomach pains, people would try to compare the stomach ache they had from gas. Or they would compare our stomach bloating. No one can compare each other's pains and symptoms because no one patient is the same.

(2014)
As you can see, I looked about 7 months pregnant here. On these days, I would get congratulated for a pregnancy that didn't exist.

(Spring 2015, 250 lbs., 36 years old)
I tried going for walks and following a healthy diet to help myself feel better. Unfortunately, my symptoms were getting worse.

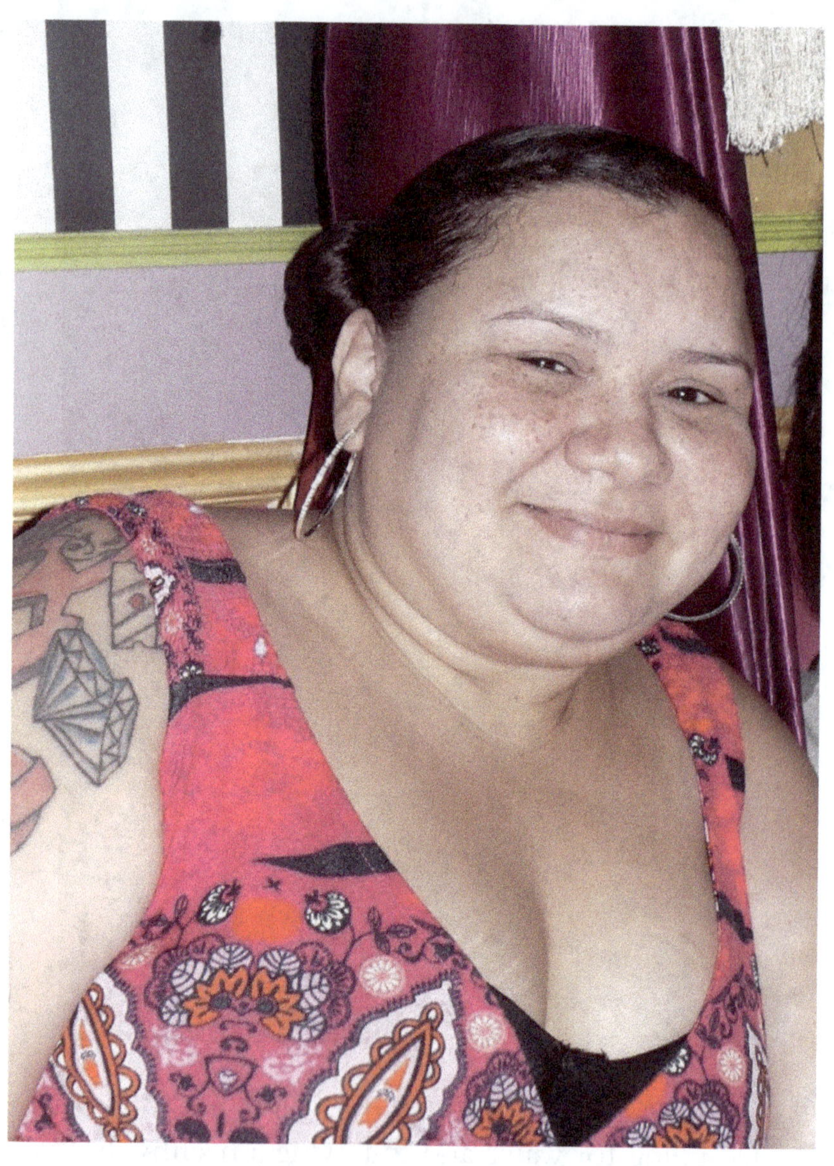

(Summer 2015, 250 lbs., 37 years old)
This was taken at my birthday dinner. I was feeling miserable but faked a smile the whole night. I couldn't even enjoy my food because I got sick.

(Summer 2015, 250 lbs., 37 Years Old)
Still struggling with my symptoms, I decided to take my children to the beach and hide how I really felt. After this, I decided to go see my doctor.

After a while, I started feeling better, so I didn't go back to the doctor until 2015. However, I was diagnosed in 2016 at the age of 37 with an incurable illness called Gastroparesis. The doctors told me they didn't exactly know where my Gastroparesis came from. At the time of my diagnosis, there wasn't much information out there about Gastroparesis. I suffered from nausea, bloating, throwing up undigested food, and stomach pains. I struggled to make it through my daily activities with how severe my symptoms ended up getting, and even though I had constant issues, that didn't stop me from eating. I was a square 270 lbs., which was the highest I have ever been.

I wanted to have a healthy relationship with food, but due to all the stressors I had in my life, all I did was constantly eat junk and unhealthy food. This is what led to all the issues I had and I wasn't educated on how I should feed my body. Most GP patients will tell you that our bodies usually love unhealthy foods and that's what leads us to being overweight, even though we are starving at times.

We are constantly being accused of being fat, lazy, that we're lying about our symptoms, that we can't be starving that badly if we are still fat, and other things that I won't honestly give any more attention to. The truth is, this couldn't be further from the truth, but unfortunately, most people won't care to educate themselves.

Now that the ability to eat properly has been taken from me, I've tried to make the best of it, and I'm sad that I missed the chance to change it. Don't be me, and please take all of this seriously. I was in denial for such a long time after my diagnosis that I made myself sicker due to all the wrong choices I was making.

I made the choice to take this seriously when I saw my family suffering. I saw them ready to bury their wife and mother. They would never tell me how they felt because they didn't want to burden me with their emotions. This is what most caregivers go through. It isn't fair, and hopefully, in reading this book, you will get the knowledge to grab hold of this illness.

I then decided in 2017 to have Gastric Bypass Surgery for my Gastroparesis. I had the hopes it would work but you have to read on to find out if it did.

It is now 2022, and I am still dealing with flare ups, nausea, and stomach aches but to what extent? Let's see…

This illness is a very lonely illness because people don't fully understand it, and a lot of times, the people going through it are called liars or sensitive. I am telling you that you are not alone, you are not a liar, this is a real illness, and the most important thing is that I BELIEVE YOU. Together, we can get through this…

CHAPTER 1

What is Gastroparesis?

Gastroparesis (GP) is an incurable illness that partially paralyzes your stomach and doesn't allow it to digest food properly. It causes food to sit in your stomach for hours, and sometimes days at a time. The symptoms are:

- Nausea
- Burping
- Bloating
- Vomiting (Sometimes you will throw up undigested food right after eating or throughout the day, especially if you eat something that doesn't agree with your stomach.)
- Regurgitation of the food you may have eaten earlier in the day or even the night before
- Pain in the stomach is possible
- Feeling fuller sooner than normal

You can also get heartburn and indigestion, especially if you eat things that you shouldn't be eating. Writing down all your symptoms and the foods you're eating will assist the doctor, along with some tests to determine what's going on. You must be very careful when trying to diagnose yourself because these symptoms can sometimes be something else. There are many illnesses and disorders that mimic GP, so please do not self-diagnose. If you're experiencing these symptoms, please go to your PCP (Primary Care Physician) with a list of your symptoms and questions you may have. He/she will then give you a referral to see a gastroenterologist. Remember that everyone's symptoms are different and range in severity.

Synonyms of Gastroparesis:

- delayed gastric emptying
- gastric atony
- gastric dysmotility
- gastric stasis
- gastrointestinal autonomic neuropathy
- gastroparesis diabeticorum
- gastropathy
- severe functional dyspepsia (NORD and Thomas Abell, n.d.)

Subdivisions of Gastroparesis:
- diabetic gastroparesis
- idiopathic gastroparesis
- post-surgical gastroparesis (NORD and Thomas Abell, n.d.)

The three stages of Gastroparesis:
There are three stages of Gastroparesis, namely; Mild Gastroparesis, Moderate Gastroparesis, and Severe Gastroparesis. Before we get into the different stages, it is important to point out that Gastroparesis affects the rate at which gastric emptying occurs. McCallum (n.d.) explains that for each of the stages, the more extreme the stage, the greater the percentage of solid food retention. Mild has less than 25% of retention, moderate ranges from 25 to 35%, while severe is usually above 35% (McCallum, n.d.).

Mild Gastroparesis:

With this stage of gastroparesis, the symptoms which I mentioned above are experienced less often (usually not on a daily basis). This also means that someone who suffers doesn't have their daily life being interrupted by it as much as someone at a more severe stage.

My research:

People with mild symptoms can lead a close to normal life. They typically can maintain their symptoms with a change in diet and lifestyle. You can still eat normally, and you may only feel some discomfort occasionally. On the other hand, you can also have severe symptoms. It all depends on the person.

Moderate Gastroparesis:
This is more severe than the mild type and the sufferer will experience symptoms more frequently—on a daily basis. However, the symptoms experienced are not constant, though one's daily life is affected negatively. Someone who has this condition will find themselves having to go to the emergency room from time to time but not too often.

My research:

I was diagnosed with Moderate Gastroparesis, and I found that in this stage, I was having difficulty digesting solid food. Purees and liquids were my best friends. I found that the foods that I considered "safe foods," were no longer safe for me to eat. The weight started dropping, but so were my energy levels. I started having difficulties with daily tasks, and I stayed in bed more often. I was going to urgent care and the emergency room more often. I also needed to rely more on medications than on diet and exercise.

Severe Gastroparesis:
This is the most severe of the three as the name suggests. The symptoms are constant—suffering is every day. It affects one's

life significantly, often making them unable to function in their daily lives with frequent hospitalizations. .

My research:

When you have severe Gastroparesis, you no longer have the ability to tolerate anything. Your stomach has almost lost all digesting ability. You also have a loss of energy, hair loss, and some persons experience muscle loss due to a lack of mobility. Additionally, due to the lack of nutrition, you may need to go on a feeding tube. I was told that my Gastroparesis was severe when I needed a feeding tube. I had a J-tube (jejunostomy tube) placed.

Disclaimer: Please remember that these are my experiences and research. Every GP patient is different and someone in the mild stage may have symptoms of someone with moderate GP.

Tests done for Gastroparesis
Gastric Emptying Study:

A 4-hour test that determines how long it takes for your stomach to digest food. The test is done by the patient getting an Xray at the beginning of the appointment. They are then given an egg with some radioactive dye in it and toast. They are given a few minutes to eat it. They then take another Xray every hour for the next three hours. Each Xray is done in a standing position.

Endoscopy:
A test that is done by putting a camera down your throat and down into your stomach. Sometimes if you have undigested food sitting in your stomach for hours, this test will be able to

see that. They will not confirm Gastroparesis this way but this test will help you on the path to diagnosis.

At this stage, you might be asking: Why does Gastroparesis suck? Well, let me tell you............

Gastroparesis will strip you of everything you love eating and doing. It will ravage your body and make you go through so many changes. Not one patient presents with the same symptoms, nor do they tolerate the same medications. Hence, why it is so difficult to manage and/or treat Gastroparesis.

Here's how I found out that I had this illness and how it changed my life in unexpected ways.

CHAPTER 2

Long Road to a Diagnosis

I was in my teenage years when I started noticing that I had stomach issues, and not your regular tummy ache either. I found that I was having problems holding down food and having pain after eating. At first, I ignored it because my biological mother never allowed me to complain when I felt sick. I had to keep that to myself. She taught me that no matter what I was going through, I should just ignore it unless I was dying. As a teenager, all you care about is hanging with your friends, if you have a crush on a person, or if you're getting good grades in school. I was uncomfortable daily with the bloating. I got tired of eating and would restrict myself for days. My biological mother didn't care, so it went unnoticed. I noticed more after I had my first son at 16. I had a smooth pregnancy but afterwards my body started feeling sick again. It's so hard to explain. I felt great during my pregnancy but right after, I started experiencing pain and suffering. I think I felt like this because I was busy worrying about my baby that I never noticed the symptoms. Well, I ignored it for so long that life flew right past me. I was in my 30s when I finally decided to take my stomach issues seriously.

If you're reading this, then I know you understand. As adults, we allow our responsibilities to pile up, and when you realize it, you are at the bottom of the pile and can't remember when the last time you took care of yourself was. With everything I had going on, I was at the bottom of the list. At this point in time, it was 2009 and I was 32.

I was a single mom of three boys and going through a separation from an abusive person, my mother-in-law and my brother-in-law had just passed away, and my children were the only light I had in the dark tunnel of life. This was when I noticed my symptoms rearing their ugly heads.

What a lot of people don't realize is that Gastroparesis is a very different illness. It is sometimes referred to as the "silent killer" in the GP community (more on this later). You could be fine for a long time, and then suddenly, out of nowhere, life hits you hard and that is when Gastroparesis comes out of hiding, like that nosy neighbor you try to get rid of but can't. The stress caused by these situations is the biggest cause of Gastroparesis flare-ups.

I went and made an appointment with my PCP to get answers to what I was going through and the symptoms I was having. All she did was give me a referral to see a gastroenterologist. "A Gastroenterologist is a physician with dedicated training management of diseases of the gastrointestinal tract and liver" (Gastroenterology Specialists of Southwest Florida, n.d.). You must remember that you will not need a referral if your insurance doesn't request it. At the time, I was on Medicaid, so I had to get a referral. I was told that it would take a few months to get in. She also informed me that I had signs of diabetes and that she wanted me to get tested for it, as it might be the cause of my upset stomach. This test was the first of many tests and procedures I had to go through with this illness. The process was easy. All I did was get my blood drawn. I then made the appointment to see the Gastroenterologist. It was scheduled for three months later.

I was so nervous about this appt. I didn't really know what to expect. I didn't really have many good experiences with doctors. The only doctor I trusted was my doctor and she had to earn that trust. The Gastroenterologist was a very tall man who I thought at the time was too perky for my taste. All I could think was that he wouldn't believe me like other doctors and that I would be left with no answers again.

We went through the introductions quickly and dove right into the problem. He told me who he was and what kind of doctor he was. He said he would get to the bottom of what was going on. All I could think was, "Yea right, PFFT. My main doctor couldn't even figure it out, and she is one of the best."

He wanted to start with some blood tests, a urinalysis, and a stool test, where you poop in a cup. He was going to test me for Crohn's, IBS, and other digestive tract illnesses. This round of tests took about two months to get all the results and wait for my doctor's appointment.

When I got there, I was optimistic that he would tell me what was wrong. Imagine my surprise when he turned around and told me, with a straight face no less, that everything "looked fine." I felt like he had literally punched me in my gut. Yet another round of normal results. Was he going to tell me that I was lying? He told me he wanted to start me on some diet changes, and we would meet again in a few months to see if that helped.

I tried the diet changes at home for a few months, and honestly, it didn't help. The vegetables were causing me to have worse pain, and the whole wheat was horrible for my intestines. Well, I didn't go back to the doctor. Who wants to go back to the doctor when all you're told is that you're fine and all your results are coming back normal? Yet I kept feeling horrible and having the same symptoms. They just kept getting worse. Think about it like this: one day you're out enjoying food, having fun, and the next day, you lose the ability to eat. You can no longer eat foods that give you comfort and bring memories of joy.

After dealing with all the tests and results, I threw myself back into my crazy life. One of the results I was told, was that I had diabetes and I had to take meds to try to manage it. That would have been great if I had been on a proper plan for whatever was ailing my stomach. I was put on Januvia, and for the next few years, it would be a rollercoaster of trying to find the proper medications to manage the high blood sugars I had. The highest my A1C got was a 9. My numbers were ranging from 180, all the way up to 300-350. Eventually, I was put on injectable insulin, and I was injecting myself in my belly area four times a day. At this point, I was between 250 lbs. and 270 lbs. I ignored the symptoms I was having, because all the tests for my stomach showed that everything was fine and I didn't want to make it seem like I was complaining. Many doctors will make you feel like you are annoying and that you can't be experiencing what you are going through because a lot of people, especially those in the medical field, don't understand that even though we are fat, we are starving and our bodies are fighting against us.

Fast forward to July 2012: I came home from work, not really feeling my best. I was having minor pains in the lower part of my chest area. At first, it started off mild, and then, out of nowhere, it took my breath away. Initially, I chucked it up to gas. Throughout the night, it got worse, so I ended up in the ER and got a CAT scan. They explained that from what they could see, my gallbladder was causing the problem and needed to be removed. They booked me into the OR and proceeded to remove my gall bladder. I went home the next day and was told to rest for 10 days then come back for a follow-up. I went back for my follow up and was told everything looked good.

A couple of months went by, and my original symptoms came back but worse. This time around, the nausea was 24 hours a day. The vomiting became worse, and I started losing weight. I was scared and frustrated because I knew I was going to have to go back to the Gastroenterologist. I tried to continue with life, and I ignored what was going on with my stomach.

Illnesses like this can cause so many problems in relationships, and hopefully, you will understand why by the end of this chapter. It can also cause you to depend on the wrong people. Who you have around you is very important because, remember, stress will make your symptoms worse. I met my soon-to-be ex-husband in 2013. I never wanted to bring someone else into this crazy life I had but something about him was different, or so I thought.

When I first started talking to him, I told him that I was sick, but I didn't know what I had. I told him I feared doctors, and that hopefully, I would muster the courage to get it all figured out. He told me he was on board, and we proceeded to date. Everything was okay for the most part (There were red flags in our relationship that should have caused me to walk away, but I didn't. Much more on that in another book.), until after our wedding in December 2014. In February, we went on our honeymoon, and I was miserable the whole time. I couldn't enjoy any food because I was constantly sick. I had to pull out of activities and stay in my room a lot of the time. My diabetes was out of control and since I didn't bring any of my meds, my sugars were in the 350's the last few days of the honeymoon plus I was in constant pain.

In 2015, I was diagnosed with Fibromyalgia, and I decided to go back to the Gastroenterologist. He was just as surprised that I was there and that I had suffered so long without coming back to him. I was known as a runner, and it was written in my files that I wasn't consistent with my appointments.

He made me promise that I wouldn't run again, and if I could do that, he would order a few more tests to see what was going on. The first test was an endoscopy. This is where they take a long hose with a camera attached to it and run it down your throat while you are either mildly sedated or fully asleep. The results were instant, and he told me he didn't see anything except for some gastritis, which is inflammation of the stomach. He was going to send some biopsies and would let me know. That would take a few weeks.

Once I finished this test, he then wanted to schedule a colonoscopy. This is where they take another hose with a camera attached to it and insert it into your butt. For this test, you must prepare at least a week or two in advance. They start you off by stopping some of the meds you are on, and then, about two days before your procedure, you must stop eating solid foods. That wasn't a problem for me since I wasn't really eating. Then, the day before your procedure, you must drink a solution to help you clear your bowels. There are different solutions you can drink, but the one he chose for me was disgusting. It was called "golytely." Again, the time it takes to do all the steps depends on the person and their situation. If you cannot tolerate liquids, then they will try something different. The results were also instant, except for the biopsies he took. He said he found diverticulosis in my intestines. Diverticulosis is a condition in which pockets in your intestines trap food and poop in them. They can cause infections and put you in a flare-up called Diverticulitis. It is a very painful infection, and the treatment is a 3-week supply of two different antibiotics. If you can't tolerate them at home, they will admit you for the duration of your treatment. Once this test was done, all I had to do was wait for all the biopsies to come back.

When the results came back, I was told that I had H-Pylori, which is an infection in your stomach. I would need to go on a strong course of antibiotics. It would be a similar course like the one for diverticulitis and it sucked heavily. Again, I needed to be admitted in the hospital because my stomach couldn't tolerate the medicine. It really sucked feeling like this and not having anyone to talk to or go through with this in my personal life. Once I was finished with the medicine, he told me he wanted to run one last test. This test would hopefully tell us what was wrong with my stomach.

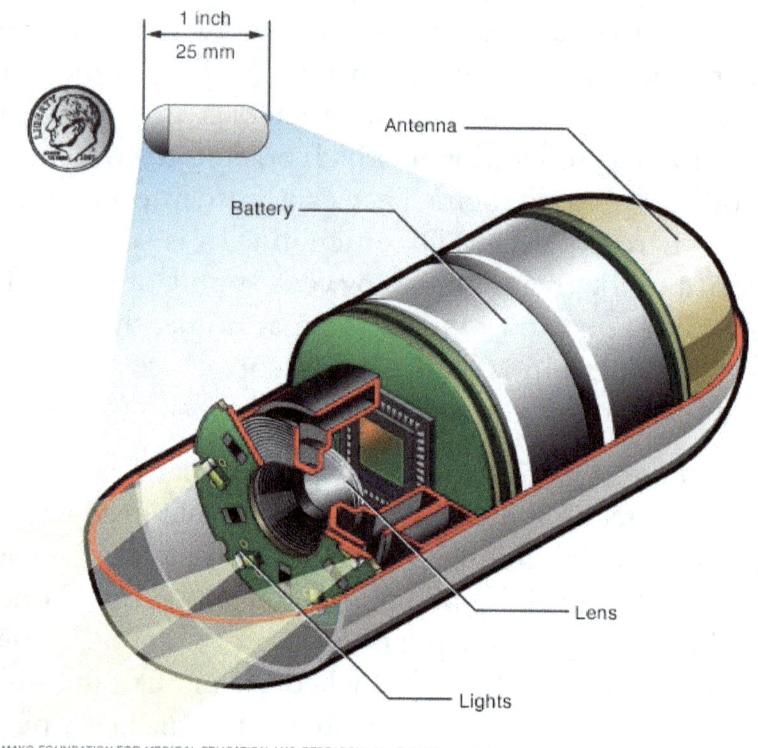

This is a camera pill. You usually swallow this if they want to do a camera endoscopy.

This test was a camera pill study. A camera pill study is where you swallow a pill camera the size of a large vitamin and it takes pictures on the way down your digestive tract. Once you swallow the pill, they make you hang a box from your neck, which then stores the pictures that the pill is taking. Here is the proper definition:

"Capsule endoscopy is a procedure that uses a tiny wireless camera to take pictures of your digestive tract" (Gastrointestinal Associates L.L.P., n.d.). A capsule endoscopy camera sits inside a vitamin-size capsule which you have to swallow. Just like food ingested, this pill will make its way through your digestive tract and as it does so, it takes photos. For the endoscopy, you get fitted with a belt that holds a recorder in it. It acts almost like a computer hard drive where the photos that the pill takes gets saved there. With those photos, the doctors are then able to see what is happening inside your small intestine.

This procedure is chosen because other endoscopy don't get to the small intestines as easily. For instance, traditional endoscopy involves passing a long, flexible tube equipped with a video camera down your throat or through your rectum (Gastroenterology Specialists of Southwest Florida, n.d.). I was then told to wait 10 days for my results. Those 10 days were the most agonizing and confusing. I must say that I was not prepared for how drastic of a change this would have on my life.

I got to my appt, I saw the doctor and he talked me through what would happen next. I would hang a little box around my neck and it would store the pictures that the camera pill would take as it travels through my digestive tract. It's supposed to travel and then you poop it out days later. They wanted me to take the pill and then go about my day. They wanted me to eat a small meal to see what happened as I eat food. The pill was not too large, I just really hate pills, so I struggled. I then went about my day and returned a few hours later to get the box analyzed. I was so anxious waiting for the results. I was telling myself that this was going to be another normal result and that doctors would think I WAS GOING CRAZY.

Are you suffering in silence?

Are you feeling unheard?

Are you scared to get tested?

Are you scared the tests might say something other than what you are feeling?

CHAPTER 3
Finally Diagnosed

(Jan 2016)
I took this picture right before I got the phone call with my
diagnosis.

In January 2016, I received a call from my doctor, who told me
that I had an illness called Gastroparesis. He explained that the
pill battery had died in my stomach, it never made it to my
intestines. It stood right in my stomach for over eight hours
from what he could see. I had the moderate type and would
have problems eating for the rest of my life. He then said I
needed a motility specialist and for me to make an appointment
within a month. He told me I needed to take this seriously and

that I needed to reach out to support groups, family, and friends. I honestly had no one. My kids were too young to lean on and my husband had the emotional range of a wall, so I was on my own.

I started off by researching what the hell GP was. I want you guys to understand that GP is a kind of new illness. In 2016, there really wasn't much information out there, and whatever was out there, was from the mouths of other patients. That would have been great, except that GP presents differently in everyone. Facebook support groups were still fairly new, and believe me when I say that when entering those rooms, you must do so with caution. They were and are full of people competing to see whose symptoms were worse, and if you offered advice or medical information, you would be cut down and told you were faking. I had to get out of there as soon as possible. I just couldn't take it.

I made an appointment with a top motility specialist in my hospital. My first appointment was at the end of April. The appointment was nerve-racking, and honestly, the specialist didn't make it any better. He started asking me questions, and with every answer I gave, he looked at me as if I was lying. I didn't feel like he believed anything I said. He explained to me that Gastroparesis was an incurable illness that could be treated with medications and diet changes. He then went on to tell me about the medications he wanted to start me off with. I was scared and confused, but I sat there and listened to the doctor while he described each medication. He wasn't a people person and it made it very hard to form a relationship with him. He didn't act like he cared and it frustrated me.

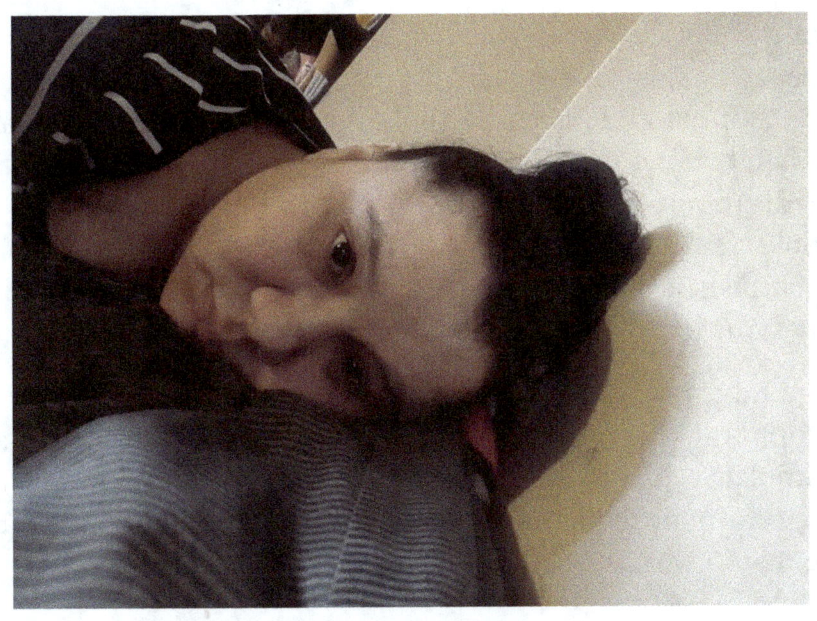

This was my face when dealing with the nasty side effects of the nasty medication I was trying.

The medications he spoke to me about were Reglan and Domperidone. Reglan was from here in the US and the other was from Canada. I decided to take Reglan because I couldn't afford the Domperidone. I was instructed to try the meds for two weeks and to come back and see him. I tried the medication for a few days and then I started seeing the side effects. I experienced really bad twitching in my face and legs. I was so scared, I stopped the medication immediately and went and did the one thing people warn you not to do… I WENT TO GOOGLE.

I then called the doctor and he also told me to stop the medication. He wanted me to try Amitriptyline instead. Amitriptyline is normally used for depression, but my doctor suggested I try it to help my digestion. I was only on that for a few days because it put me in a zombie-like state, where I was completely out of it for a few days. I threw the meds away because I was tired of feeling that way. I would spend at least 12+ hours in bed because the medication would make me feel sedated and out of it. I spent about a month trying these medications: About two weeks on each medication, so that I could feel like I gave it a try. I went back to my motility specialist because the medications weren't working at all, and my symptoms were getting worse.

At this point, I weighed about 240 lbs. and my weight started dropping drastically. He recommended having a gastric stimulator placement done. So now I needed to make an appointment with the surgeon and start researching what the next step was.

CHAPTER 4

Needing a Support Team and a Caregiver

After my diagnosis, I had to take a second to figure out what to do. The first person I reached out to, of course, was my husband. I thought that he would be there for me, but boy was I wrong. The first thing he did was turn his back on me. He treated me like a burden. He started ignoring me; he would never be there for me, and he told me he had fallen out of love with me because I had gotten sick. I was heartbroken, and I felt like it was my fault. I was hurt. I felt disrespected, unloved, and alone. However, I didn't let that knock me down. I pushed through and started looking for other support systems that could help me.

I knew I couldn't lean on my kids because they were too small, so I did what the doctor recommended and went looking for groups that might be able to help me. I went straight to Facebook and typed in "Gastroparesis" into the search bar. A few groups popped up and I clicked on all of them. I will be honest with you and say that I wasn't prepared for the stuff I saw or heard. I will give you a fair warning and tell you to enter at your own risk. Everyone's experiences are different, and you may not like what you see. Just as quickly as I entered, I made my way out. The groups were full of drama and fights. Everyone was in competition with each other. The people who truly needed help were being drowned out by those who only wanted attention. I felt that those groups were only making me sicker.

I didn't really have friends before my diagnosis, so I didn't have to worry about people not being my friend anymore. I did find a few good people in the groups, and they became my support system. Christina, Allison, and a few other people became family to me. They were the support I needed online.

As I got sicker, I started losing the ability to bathe myself, dress myself, or even get out of bed. I had to hire a home attendant who would take care of me daily and be paid through my insurance. This woman would work six hours a day, five days a week. She would bathe me, dress me, clean the house for me, and help me to my appointments. She was the best thing to happen to me while I was sick. She was a mother figure to me and I really depended on her to give me the love and care I needed.

Side Note: If there is no one that is willing to take care of you, then let your insurance know and they might be able to get you a home attendant.

Once I got that settled, I set the appointment with the surgeon for the placement of the gastric stimulator. The appointment was set for about three months away at the end of July 2016.

CHAPTER 5
Gastric Stimulator

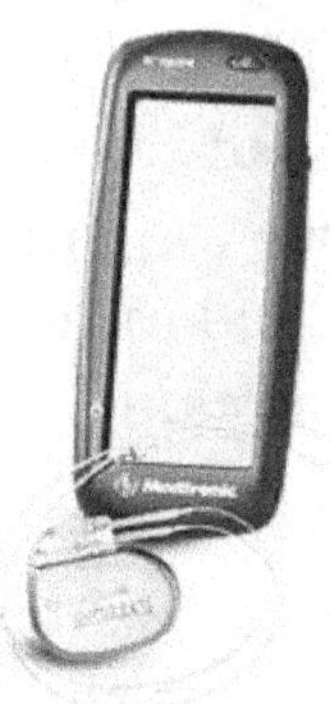

(Jun 26, 2016)

This is a Gastric Stimulator. This is the Enterra Brand.

Here's a description of what a gastric stimulator is so that you can understand what I'm talking about when it comes to the stimulator itself. A gastric stimulator is a small electrical machine that is placed surgically in your belly area right under your skin. It is about 3 inches wide and about 2 inches high. It is turned on by a handheld machine that is held in the doctor's office and will be modified by said machine at every doctor's appt you have until you find a setting that works.

It can take a few trips for you to get to the proper setting that will work for you. You must remember that not one GP patient experiences the exact same symptoms, so each stimulator must be uniquely set for each patient. I was told it would help me eat again and that I wouldn't feel it. He said that it would be adjusted based on how I tolerated food. The battery is said to last anywhere from 3 to 5 years, depending on how strong you need the setting to be.

On June 7th or 8th of 2016, I ended up in the emergency room for the first time with severe dehydration, and I had not eaten or drunken anything in about three days. I couldn't hold anything down and my blood sugars were in the 50s because I was a diabetic. I literally felt like I was dying. I was so scared. This was the first time I had to experience how patients with GP are treated. Before they took me seriously, they treated me like a drug addict. They asked me a million questions about my medications and if I was seeking any pain meds because they wouldn't give me any.

I had to cry and refuse any pain meds I felt I needed just so that they would have a proper conversation about the symptoms I was having. They made me wait hours to see if I would have a change of heart. I finally got to see a doctor who was wonderful and listened to my every word. He hooked me up to IV fluids, gave me Zofran for my nausea, and ordered some tests to see what was going on. I was then admitted to the hospital so that they could come up with a plan.

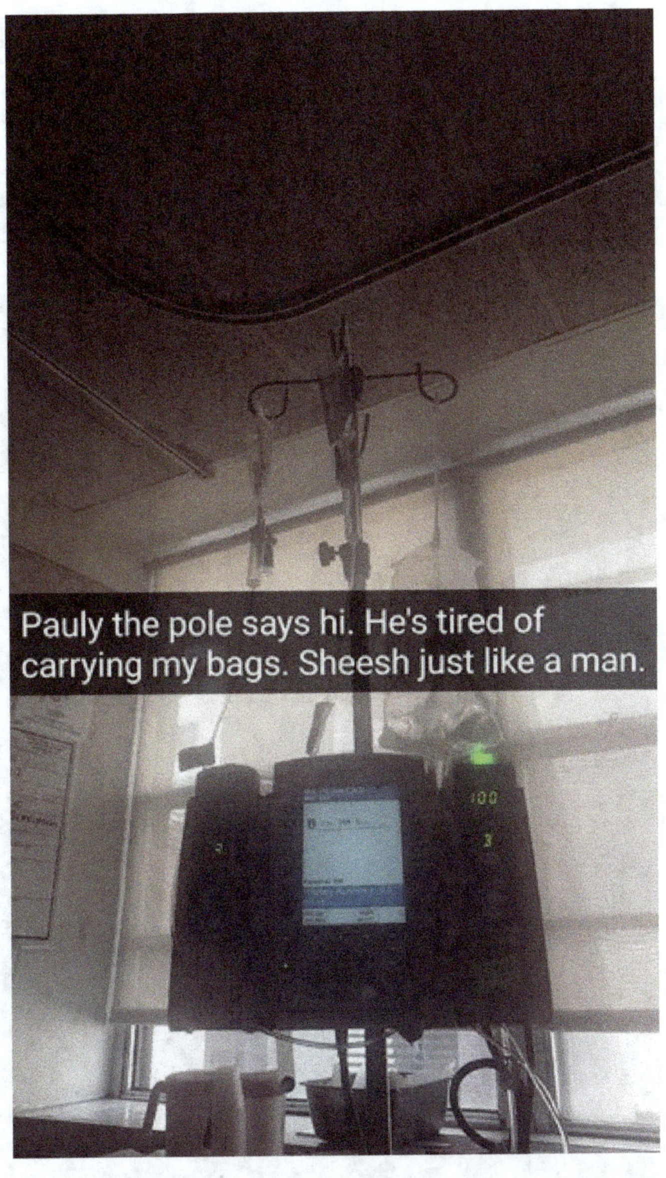

I tied to make the best out of my time at the hospital by taking videos and pics during my stay.

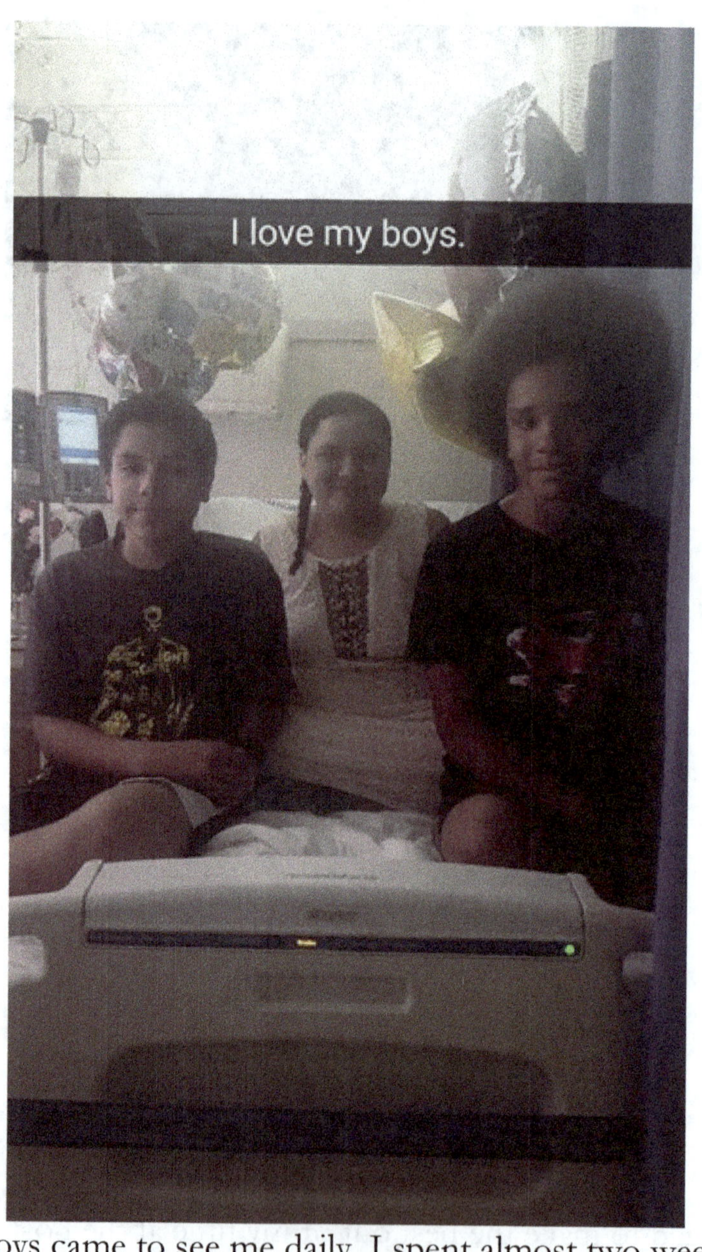

My boys came to see me daily. I spent almost two weeks in the hospital.

The way I was treated in the hospital was horrible, and it wasn't even the nurses who did it. It was the doctors and the residents that treated me like I was lying because most of my blood test results were normal. As I sat there in my hospital bed, suffering in silent agony because I felt unheard and alone, I wondered what my life would turn into. I wondered if this was the way people were going to view me and this ugly illness. I found out a few days into my stay that they had no real plan and that they were waiting for my surgical doctor—whom I had never met—to come and decide what was going to happen to me. Luckily for me, the next day, I got to meet the surgeon.

Little did I know that this surgeon would be my biggest supporter and ally in my fight to be heard about a silent illness that was slowly killing me, or at least that's what it felt like it was doing. She started by asking me how I felt and what my symptoms were exactly. She heard everything I had to say and did not interrupt me once. She looked excited and optimistic about what she recommended the plan to be. She left the decision up to me and made sure to give me all the important information I needed to make a proper decision.

I was shocked at the fact that she had such amazing bedside manners and that she wasn't looking at me like I was crazy. For the first time, I felt heard, and I was excited to see what this new piece of equipment would do for me. I decided to go through with the surgery and it was booked for the next morning. I had been in the hospital for about two weeks before they came and spoke to me about surgery. This had to be done quickly and this was hopefully going to save me from literally starving to death.

They came and got me early in the morning and brought me downstairs. The surgery lasted about 90 minutes. I was in recovery when I woke up, and I felt great. I was taken to my room about an hour after that. My surgeon visited me and asked me a ton of questions. She asked me what my pain level was, whether I was nauseous or not, and if I was feeling the machine. I was asked to try and eat something. It was crackers. I was excited because for the first time, I ate something and didn't get nauseous. I know you're probably thinking, "But it was only crackers." But if you don't have this illness, you won't understand that even crackers can make us sick for days.

She then told me, if I could hold it down, I could go home later that evening. After a couple of hours, I was allowed to go home under some restrictions. They made an appointment for me to see the motility specialist and get the stimulator adjusted in a few days. I was excited and scared because this would be the first time in months that I wouldn't feel nauseous, or I wasn't throwing up my food. I went to my first appointment and got the stimulator adjusted. It was a painless process. All I had to do was lie there while the doctor brought the machine close to my stimulator. He pressed a few buttons and then told me he was done. Honestly, he didn't really explain much to me, and it was frustrating.

I went home with high hopes that this would work. I did everything the doctor told me. I changed my eating habits. I ate only healthy foods like broccoli and salads, and I cut out red meat. Everything was going well, and I was so happy. It only lasted a couple of weeks, though. Out of the blue, I ended up with all my symptoms again. I felt horrible and scared. I went back to the doctor, and he told me all he would have to do was adjust the machine and it should work again. Well, let me tell you that it never went back to the way it was for those couple of weeks. If anything, I got worse and at a faster rate.

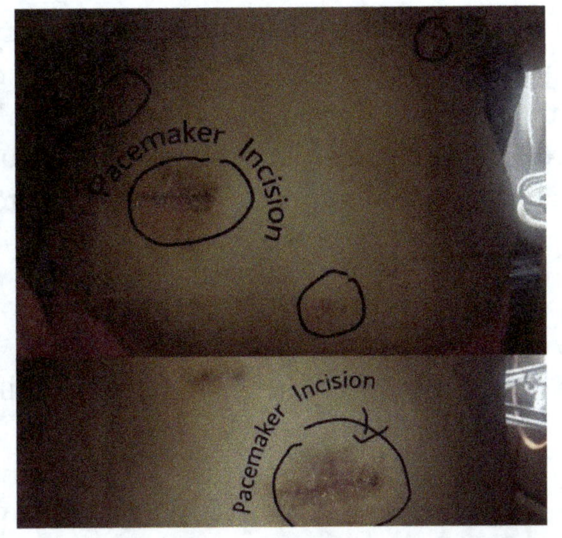

These are the incisions that are made for the tools to insert the stimulator. The larger slit is where the device and wires go. Think of it like a little pocket. It holds the device that sends signals to your stomach so it can start digesting.

I don't know if it was the stress or the fact that I went back to eating unhealthily, but things just kept going downhill. Any person who suffers from Gastroparesis will tell you that our body will be okay with unhealthy foods, but the moment we try to eat vegetables or anything healthy, we become bloated, we throw up, and are sick in bed all day. This continued for months. I felt like I was back to square one and I was scared of what the future held for me. Life as I knew it was over, and this new scary life was beginning. I couldn't be a mother, a wife, and most importantly, I couldn't be myself.

We then tried Botox injections. Yes, you read that right, Botox injections. If you have ever seen a picture of the stomach, you will notice it has a top and bottom opening of sorts. The bottom one is the pylorus and for those of us who suffer with gastroparesis, what happens is that this is affected, thus impacting the food retention process which was described when I explained the different stages earlier. In actuality, the rate at which food is emptied from the stomach is affected (digestion). With Botox, the pylorus is able to relax, thus impacting the digestive process positively—food gets emptied faster from the stomach. I was told that it would last for up to three months and that if it worked, I could get these shots every 3-6 months if needed but that it was only a temporary fix. I had Botox done a total of two times. I didn't like it and it didn't work. It's a simple procedure just like an endoscopy. They put you in a light sleep so that they could inject the medication into your pylorus.

Unfortunately, at the end of November, things took a turn for the worst. My body stopped tolerating food and liquids. I lost 40 lbs. in 3 weeks, and I couldn't dress myself, or walk without assistance. My body felt like it was shutting down. I was scared and I literally thought that I was going to die. I went and saw my motility specialist for the last time. I begged him to help me because I couldn't continue living the way I was. Nothing that he had recommended had worked for me. I was literally starving to death, and I was willing to do whatever it took for me to feel better. He referred me back to my surgeon so that I could get a J-tube put in my intestine. A J-tube is one type of feeding tube. I will explain more about the different types of feeding tubes in the next chapter.

> *Are you thinking about getting the Gastric Stimulator?*
>
> *If you are, please make sure that you do your research and ask a lot of questions. I wish I would have researched more because it would have saved me a lot of lost time.*

CHAPTER 6
The Different Types of Feeding Tubes

What are feeding tubes and why do you need them?

I took this definition from Wikipedia as that was where I was able to develop my understanding better. Essentially, "A feeding tube is a medical device used to provide nutrition to people who cannot obtain nutrition by mouth" (Wikipedia, n.d.). With food being one of our basic need, it's a given that one has to consume it. However, as you know, often times, people cannot eat naturally for different reasons whether it has to do with their inability to swallow or something else. Feeding tubes are made from materials like silicone and polyurethane to help these people "eat" instead—though they are not ONLY for consuming food. Being fed through a feeding tube will usually be referred to as one of three terms; i.e., tube feeding, gavage or enteral feeding. Placement may be temporary for the treatment of acute conditions or lifelong in the case of chronic disabilities.

The Different Types of Feeding Tubes
There are a few different types of feeding tubes. The starter tubes are the nasal tubes. They are meant to be temporary and are placed by an x-ray technician. They are used to give you nutrition, push your meds through, clean out the contents of your stomach, and flush fluids through. Then you have the more permanent tubes that are surgically placed either in your stomach or intestine. They serve the same function as temporary tubes. Then you have PICC lines that are placed in the arm and need to be taken care of more carefully. PICC lines are the last options and are dependent on your situation.

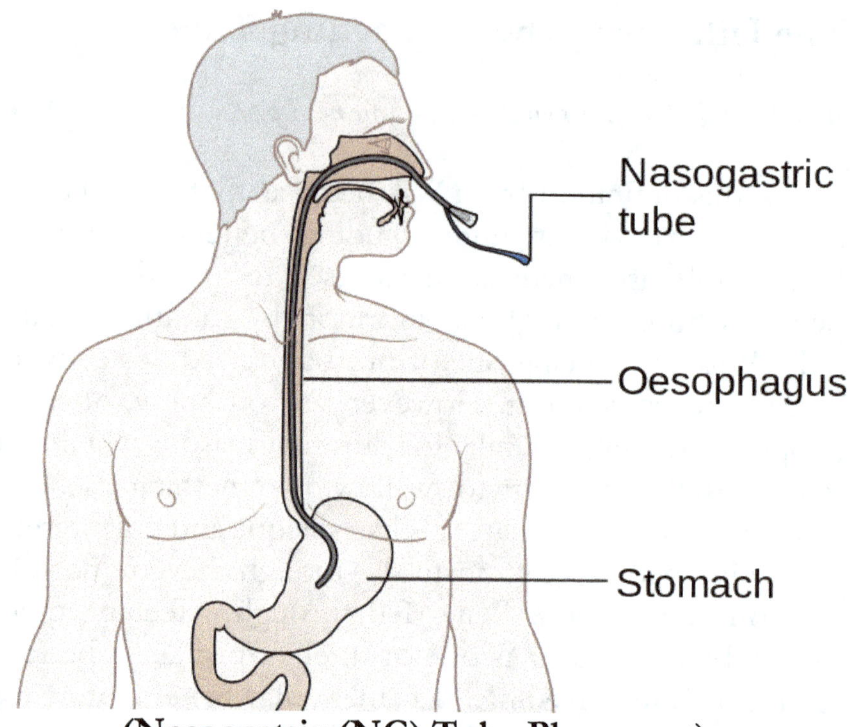

(Nasogastric (NG) Tube Placement)
The tube travels through the nose down the esophagus and into the stomach.

NG

Feeding tubes can be inserted in different ways, however, the Nasogastric (NG) intubation is inserted in one's nose. It is a thin plastic tube traveling from your nose (usually up one of your nostrils) into your esophagus and then into your stomach. As much as it can be used to feed someone, it can also be used for taking medicines. Additionally, it can be used to remove things from the stomach—from taking samples of what's inside the stomach to getting rid of things that are harmful to it.

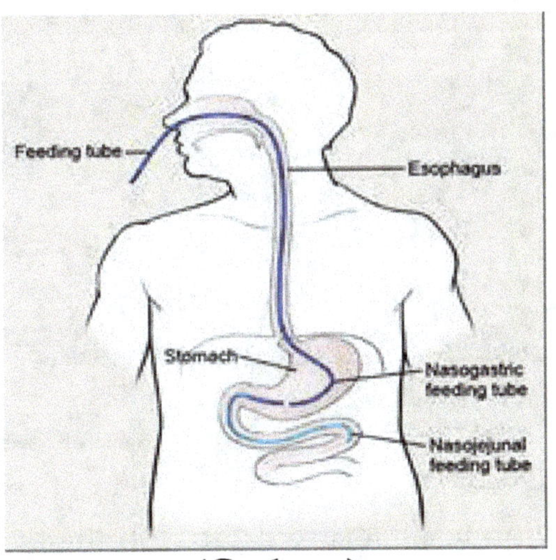

(Gralapp)

The tube travels through the nose, down the esophagus and into the stomach.

NJ

Like the NG, this tube goes through the nose as well in order to get to the stomach. Known formally as a nasojejunal (NJ) tube, it is thin and soft. Eventually, it ends up in the jejunum which is inside the small intestine. Like many other tubes, it is used to give you food and medicine.

Surgically Placed Tubes

G-tube

This tube gets into the stomach through the abdomen. An incision is usually made on the left side of the abdomen (upper) for the tube to be inserted into. One is able to "eat" without ingesting any food via their mouth. Fluids and medicine can also be had through this tube.

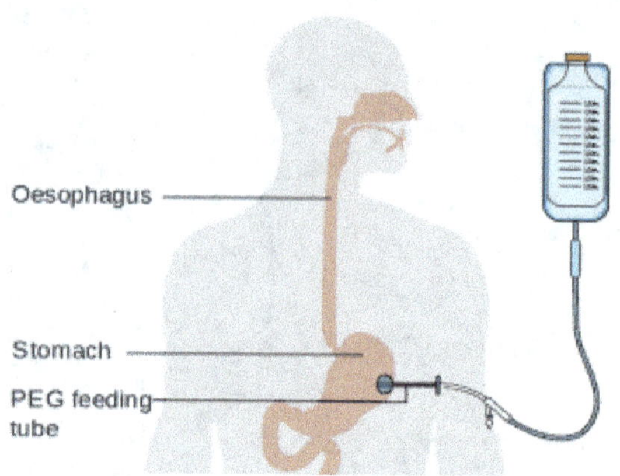

The tube is surgically inserted through the belly area into the intestine.

J-tube

This tube is placed through an incision in the abdomen that is lower than the G-tube placement. Like the NJ, it allows access to the jejunum. It is smaller than the G-tube. Unlike some of the other tubes, it cannot accept food. Only thin liquids can go through it and in terms of medications, it is usually in the form of finely grounded powder.

For extreme situations, there are PICC lines placed.

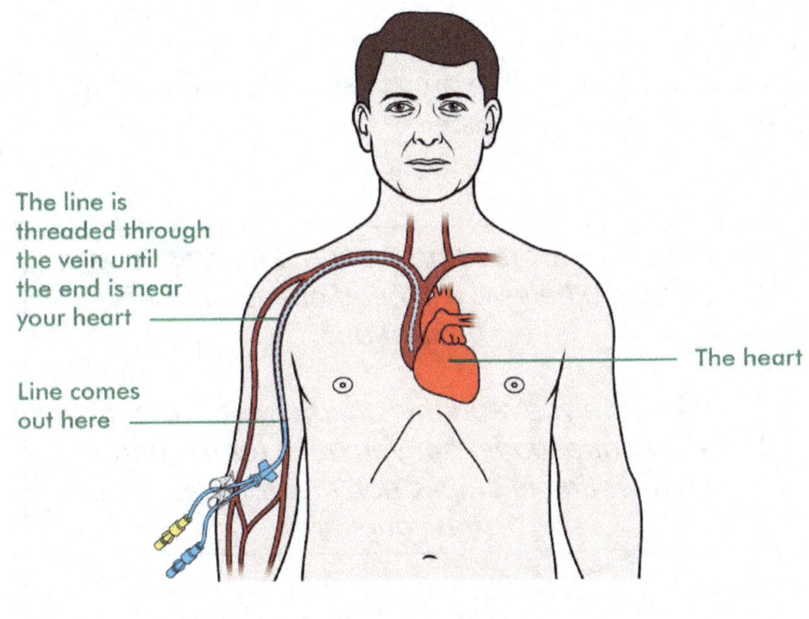

(PICC lines)

<u>PICC Lines</u>
A PICC line is a longer catheter that's also placed in the upper arm. The tip of the PICC ends up in the largest vein of the body. This is why it is considered a central line. PICC stands for "peripherally inserted central-line catheter" (Demarco, 2018).

You will receive TPN (total parenteral nutrition) through the PICC Line. This simply means that the gastrointestinal tract is bypassed. Fluids are inserted through a vein to provide most of the nutrients the body needs. People who cannot ingest food by the mouth usually uses this—or people who shouldn't consume food this way for one reason or another. You will also receive any meds you need through this same line.

A PICC line is only placed if all other methods have not worked. They will attempt other methods before this one.

This next part of the story will be bloody and gross. It will be real and raw. I will be going into detail about what it was like to live with a J-tube. If you get sick from blood or pus, then please skip this next chapter.

Is your doctor recommending a feeding tube or do you believe you need one to help with nutrition?

Make sure you read this chapter and write down all the questions that you have for the doctor. No question is stupid, don't let anyone tell you that yours are.

CHAPTER 7
Life with a J-tube

The motility specialist referred me back to my surgeon so that I could get a J-tube put in my intestine.

I saw the surgeon within a couple of days, and unfortunately, she couldn't perform the surgery, so she asked her colleague to do it. The surgery was scheduled for a week later, and I was admitted to the hospital in the meantime so that I could get IV nutrition. The surgery was scheduled for the afternoon, and it took a total of 90 minutes. I woke up in recovery in an immense amount of pain and was very regretful of what I had done. I looked down and I had a red tube sticking out of me attached to my skin with stitches. I couldn't believe how awful it looked, but I was told this would help me get the nutrition I needed.

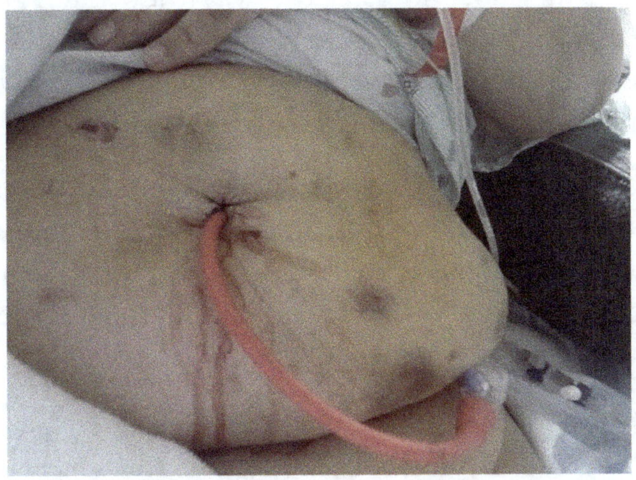

This red rubber tube was stitched to the left side of my belly area. It went directly into my intestine. It didn't have a balloon on the inside to hold the tube in place, like other tubes had, so anytime it moved, it had to be stitched in place and yes, it was as painful as it looks.

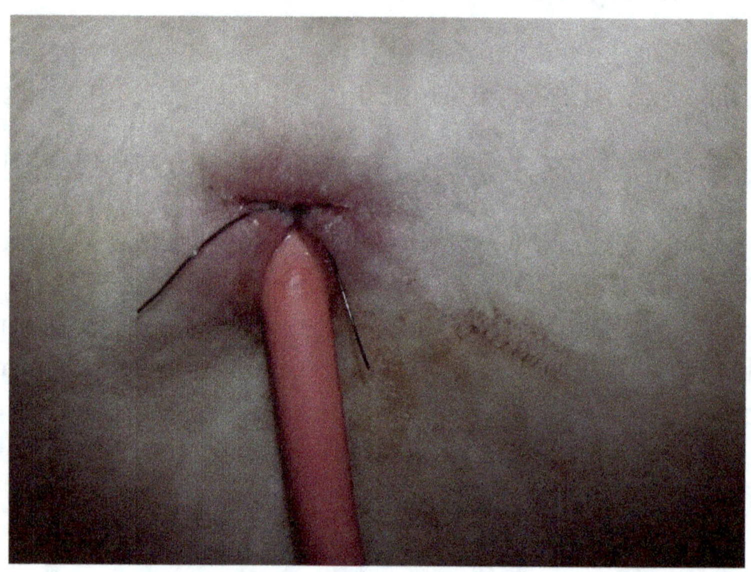

This is an up-close look at the way they stitch these types of tubes. It was very painful and it wasn't secure. I felt it constantly tug and pull. I could barely move and doing daily things were difficult.

The next morning, after surgery, a nurse came into my room to educate me on taking care of my feeding tube. I had to now learn how to take care of this thing sticking out of my body that was now going to be feeding me for the foreseeable future.

The lessons she taught me were:
- Hygiene on my part
- Cleaning of the tube
- Flushing the tube before and after feedings
- Rate of feeds
- Starting and stopping feeds

- Pushing meds through the tube
- What to do if stitches come undone or balloon of water deflates
- What to do for clogs
- Securing the tube to your skin with the proper adhesive

Imagine having to wrap your head around not just having something now hanging from your belly, but you must also learn how to care for it within a matter of hours because they want you to go home and not take up space that can be given to someone who is more ill. I will break down each lesson so that if you're looking into getting a feeding tube, you will be aware of the things you will have to learn to care for it. Let's start with:

Hygiene on your part:
Taking care of a feeding tube isn't as easy as just washing it out. You must have a sterile environment because you don't want to get an infection. You have to make sure you have alcohol pads, all the tools that you need, like syringes, gauze, etc., and gloves to put on. Once everything has been organized, you can then proceed to get the feeding bag ready to attach to the machine.

You begin by filling the bag with the formula that you were given at the time you were in hospital. You then hang the bag from an IV pole and run the hose part of the bag through the machine. Turn on the machine and start it so that the air can run through the hose and the formula can start moving through it. After this, allow some formula to run through the hose end to ensure there is no air in the hose. Then press the pause button on the machine so that you can clean your tube.

My experience

This was the scariest thing I had to do. I wanted to make sure I listened and took as many notes as I could. Unfortunately, the nurse teaching me didn't have the patience to stop and go over what I didn't understand.

Cleaning of the tube:

Gather your gloves, alcohol swabs, syringes filled with water, gauze pads, tubie covers, and, if necessary, any meds that you may need to take. Put your gloves on and get your alcohol wipes. Start wiping the end of your tube once you open the cover. Then pick up your syringe and flush your tube to check for clogs or tears. After you make sure it isn't clogged or torn, you can attach the feeding tube and proceed to restart the machine you attached the feeding bag to. They then set your feeds at a very slow rate and watch for pain, cramping, and bloating. If you do not experience any these in 24 hours, they will then raise your rate. They will continue doing this for a couple of days until it gets to a comfortable rate for both the doctor and you.

Flushing tube before and after feeds:

It is very important to flush before and after feeds. You should do it before to check for any clogs or tears. You don't want to start feeds and have it shoot right back at you. Believe me, it isn't cute. You should also do it after to clean out the feeds that were running through it. You wouldn't want to leave formula in the tube for too long because then it starts to stink and gunk up. It's the most disgusting thing I have ever smelled. Flush with filtered water all the time. Tap water might be too dirty and you don't want harmful bacteria in your tube. I mean, it's already sitting in your intestine; you don't want any more nasties in there.

Rate of Feeds:

The hospital will help you set your rate of feeds while you are there. Every set is different for each person. The rate of feeds depends on how well you tolerate the pressure of the formula going through your intestines. The less you tolerate, the slower the feeds will be. The better you tolerate the feeds, the higher the rate. You need to be completely honest with your doctor because if you don't, he will set your rate at what he/she feels is best. I couldn't really tolerate feeds at first and I was too embarrassed to say anything, so the doctor set it at a high rate and the pain it caused is something I can't really explain. I learned my lesson, and from that point on, I was always honest with my team.

Starting and stopping feeds:

If you are on 24-hour feeds, this is not for you. Everyone will get a set time they have to be attached to their feeds and it will differ per person. Mine was set at 12 hours a day because it was hard for me to tolerate the formula. I set the machine to know when to exactly start and stop, but if you feel any type of pain and/or bloating, you can manually stop the feeds yourself. You can also restart whenever you feel better. Don't force yourself to continue through any discomfort because all you're doing is hurting yourself.

Pushing meds through the tube:

You will also have to push your meds through your tube. If your stomach isn't digesting food or liquids, then there will be no way that your body can absorb any type of meds. Your doctor will tell you which meds can be crushed up and pushed through the tube with water. Not all meds can be crushed up. Extended-release medications are not crushable and can't be pushed through the tube. When pushing meds through your tube, you want to crush the meds into a fine powder and mix with water until the medicine dissolves. Then fill the syringe with liquefied medicine and push it right through the tube. Be very careful with the dosage because since you are pushing it through your intestine, you will feel the effects immediately.

<u>What to do if stitches come undone or balloon of water deflates</u>:

You may run into a problem with your tube. It depends on how your tube was inserted and placed. The tube I had was attached to my skin by stitches. Other tubes are held by a balloon positioned on the inside of the belly and inflated with water. Due to mine being attached by stitches, it became stuck to my clothes and the adhesive I put on my skin quite easily. My stitches came undone a few times and the tube started coming out. Every time it happened, I had to go to the emergency room to get it restitched. It was a painful process, and I hated going through it. I've heard of tubes slipping completely out and having to get the tube inserted back in. It was said that the techs who performed the procedure were insensitive and caused more pain.

Sometimes the balloon can deflate by losing water slowly. You can refill the balloon yourself by filling a small syringe with water and attaching it to a small hole in the balloon. Then you push the liquid in. If you can't refill the balloon, you must go to the ER and get it filled there.

<u>What to do for clogs</u>:

If your tube spits out the water or formula, then your tube might be clogged. You can test the tube by trying to push warm water slowly through the tube. If you feel that you are forcefully pushing the liquid through, then your tube is clogged, and you should call your doctor. He might tell you to come in and get your tube replaced.

<u>Securing the tube to your skin with the proper adhesive</u>:

You must secure your tube to your skin so that it won't get snagged on anything. I found that my skin was very sensitive to many tapes. I went through so many before I found a surgical tape that worked wonderfully. There are many types out there and you will have to do your own research to find the one that works for you.

This is what my new life looked like:

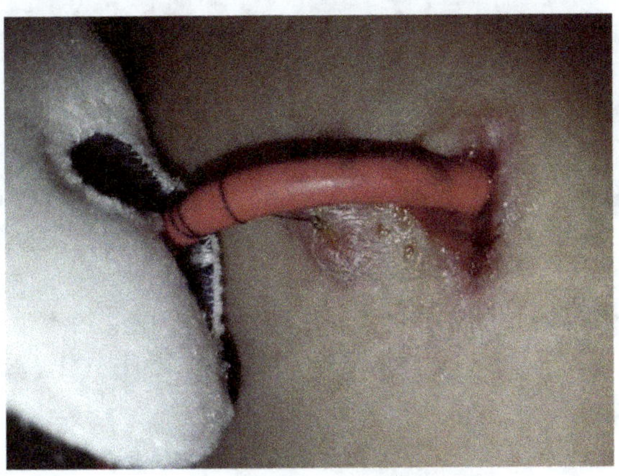

(December 2016)
This was my new tube. It was a red rubber hose with no closing. I had to insert something in the opening until I got the proper head in it.

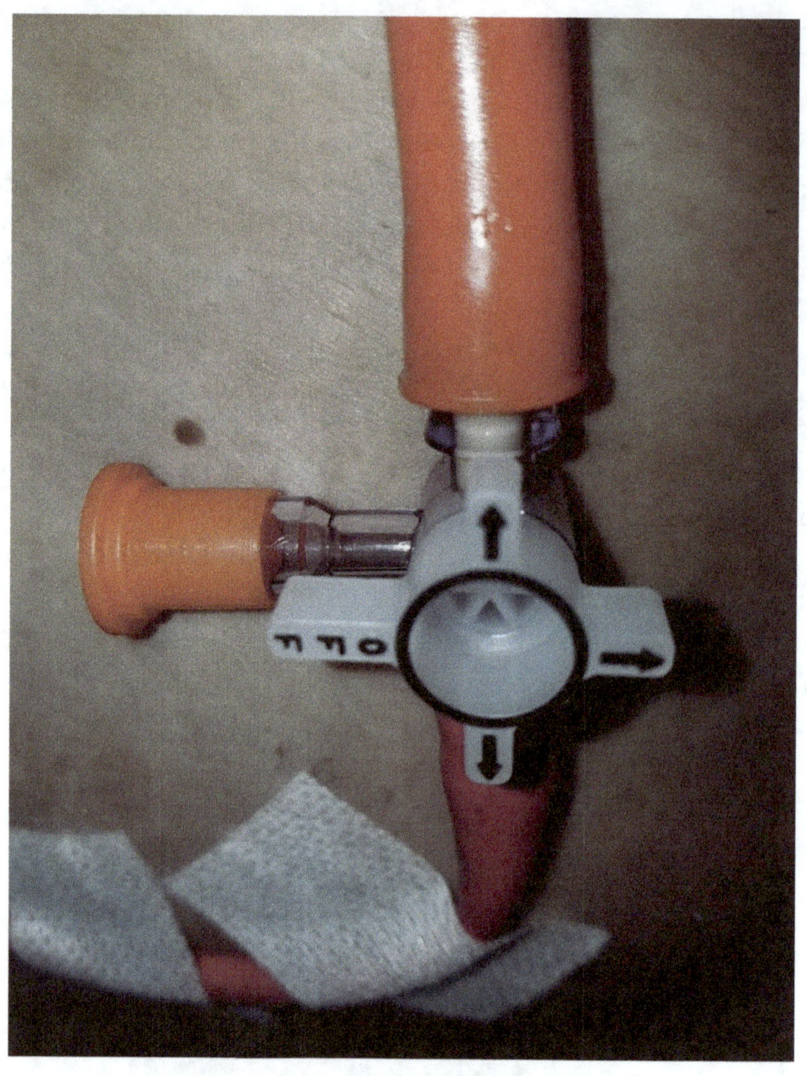

This was the hose once I had the proper head in the tube with the valve button to stop the flow so that I could clean it.

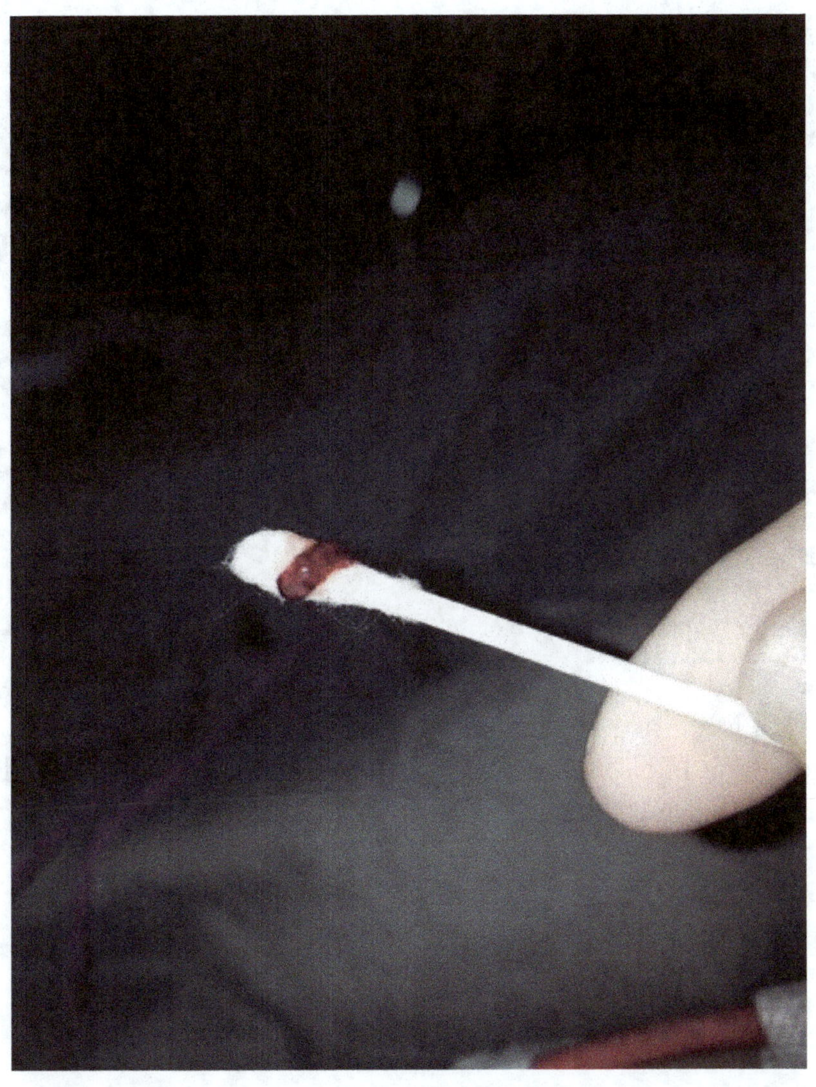

These were small clots that would come from my tube whenever I cleaned it. My tube bled constantly and it moved a lot.

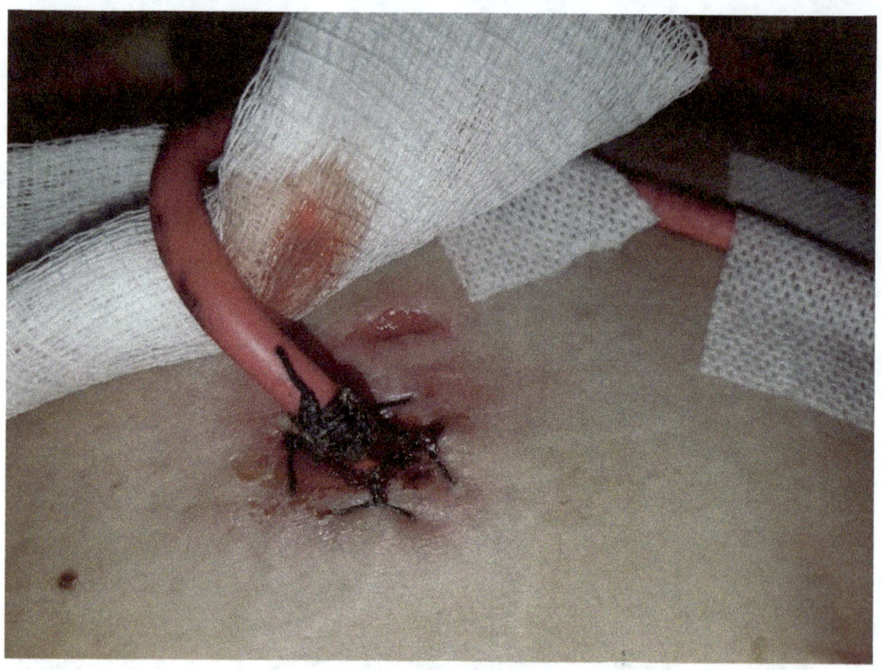

This is a close up of the tube. this is the thread that they use to sew it back in position when it slips out. These threads rip through your skin. If this rips, it will have to be sewn back in.

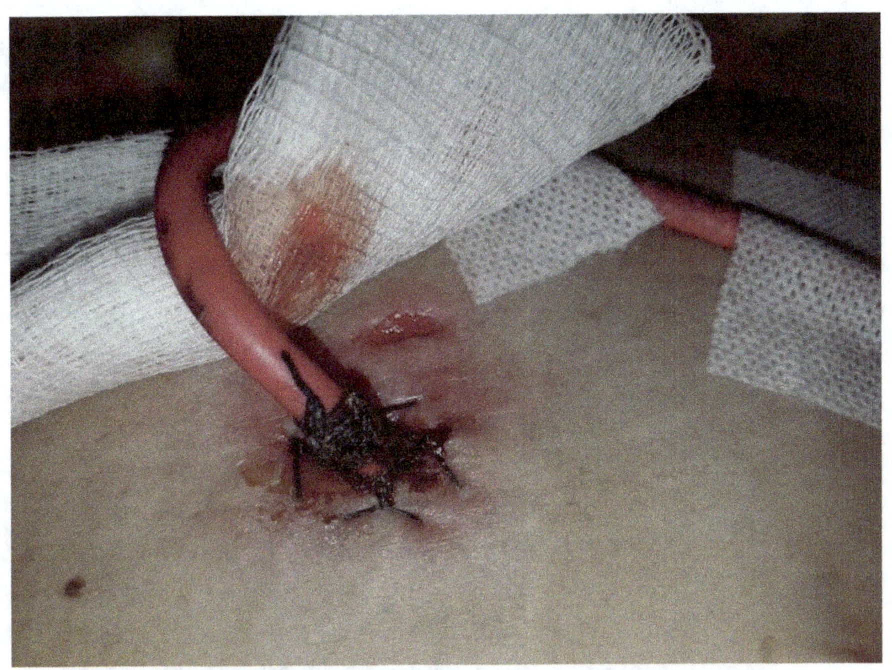

This is pus and blood coming out of the hole where the tube is attached. This has to be cleaned frequently throughout the day.

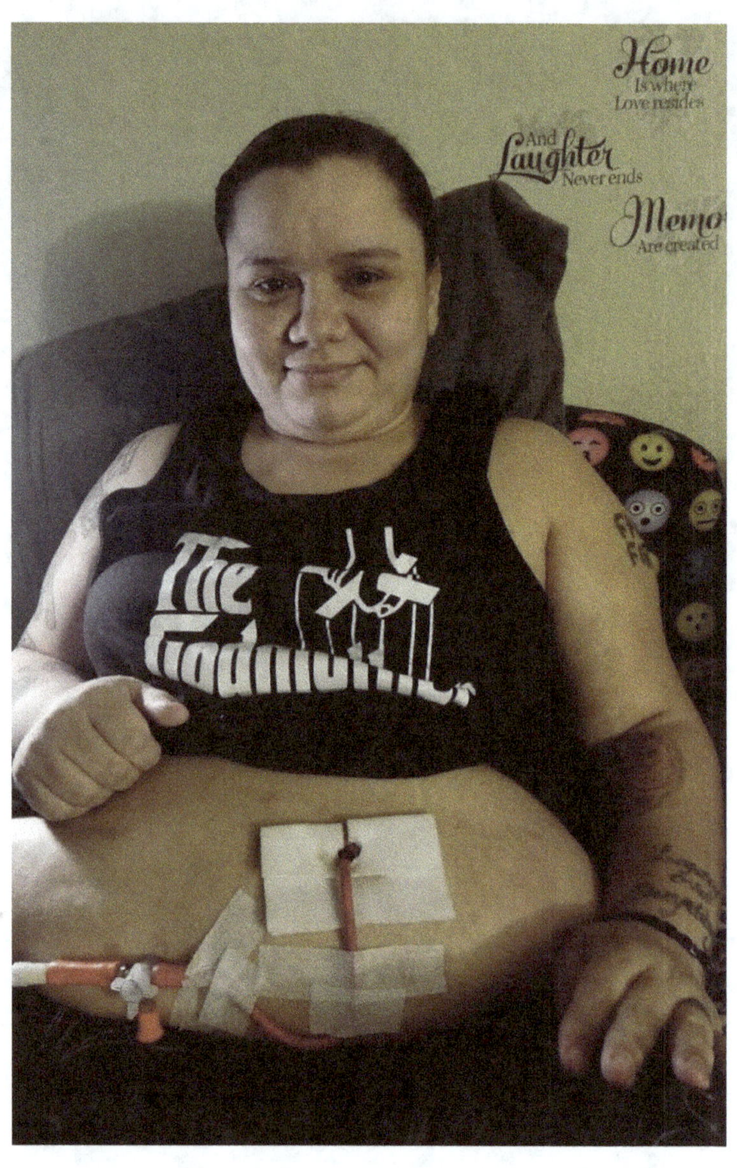

I decided to take this picture of my tube and I because I wanted to show myself that there was nothing to be scared of. I wanted to show people that were thinking about getting it that they weren't alone.

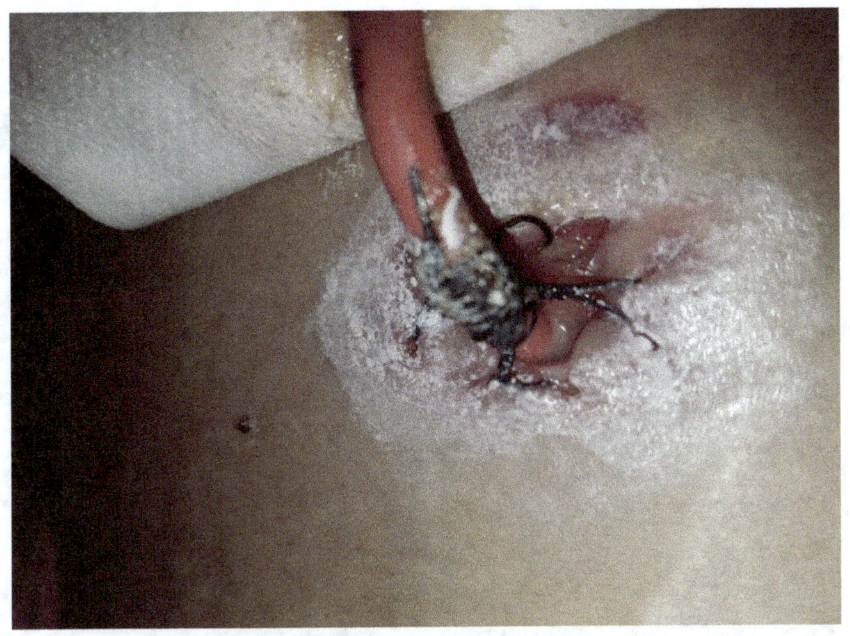

Here is closer look at the tube before it gets cleaned. You have to constantly clean the tube to ensure that you don't get an infection.

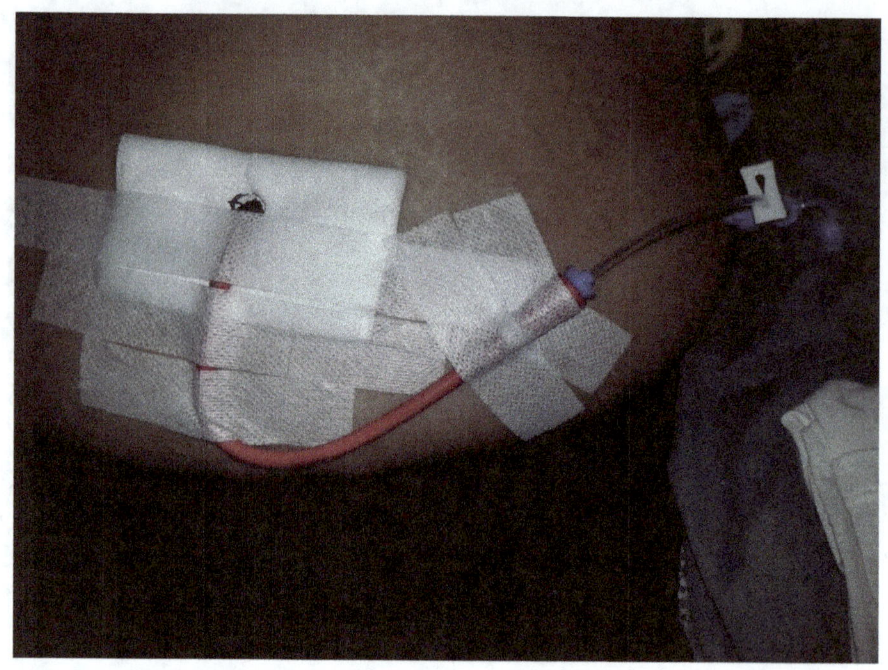

This is how I taped the tube to my skin. My skin would get very irritated and I would get bad rashes due to the different tapes I had to use.

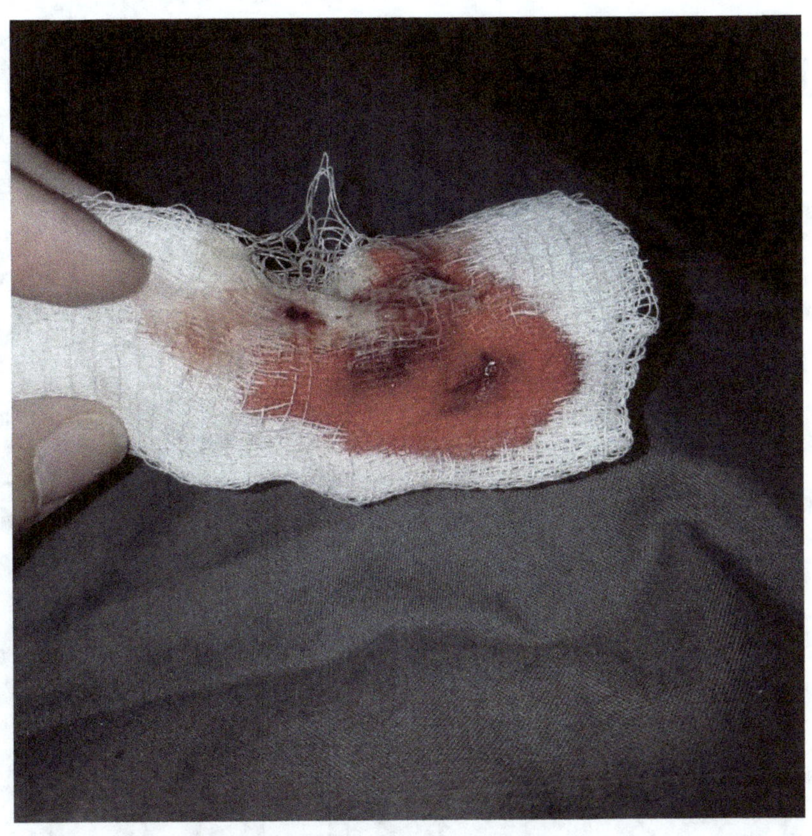

This is what all my gauzes looked like a few times a day. I cried daily because I was scared. I reached out to my doctors and was told that this is normal. This is unfortunately normal for those whose body is rejecting the tube.

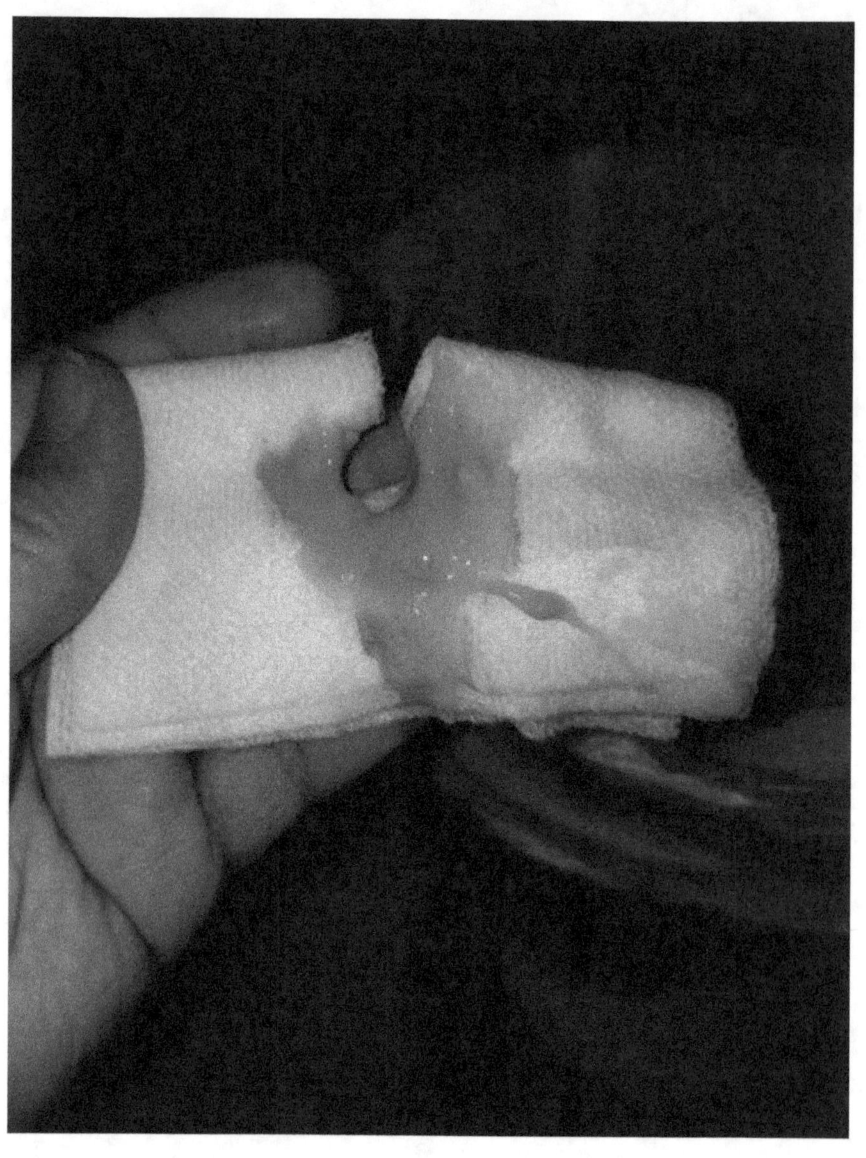

I'm showing a lot of these gauzes so that the seriousness of feeding tubes is understood. This is what happens with most feeding tubes.

They don't tell you how difficult it is to live with a feeding tube. Yes, the tube is meant to save your life, but no one tells you how hard it is and how much you are going to hate a lot of the aspects of it. I had a love-hate relationship with my tube. It was disgusting and it smelled. My stitches popped a few times, and I had to go to the ER to get it restitched. Pus constantly flowed from the hole in my belly. I ran out of gauze quickly and the tube covers were not absorbent enough to hold the amount of pus that was coming out of the hole. There were times that I would fall asleep, and my formula would run out, so my tube would fill my intestine with air. It was so painful and it caused me to look pregnant.

I was stressed about the tube and the relationships around me failing. My husband reminded me constantly that he didn't sign up for this life. He made me feel like a burden, and he didn't like having to take care of me. We argued all the time because he thought I was faking. He said he couldn't believe that I was in pain the way I said I was. I had to take care of myself, and it made me fall into depression. He made me get a home attendant because he said that he shouldn't have to take care of me. I literally had to prove to him that I was as ill as I was telling him that I was. I felt like no one believed me, and often wondered what the point of fighting was if everyone made me feel as if I was better off dead. I know I'm not the only one that felt this way, and I need you to know that it will get better. Don't allow yourself to fall into negative self-talk. Don't kick yourself because you're not feeling better fast enough, or you need more bed days than others.

As for my children, they were younger, and they tried their best to help me, but they were still children after all, and I wasn't going to allow them to get swallowed up by the sadness this illness brought with it. I didn't really let my children know how bad my situation was. I didn't want them to worry about me, so I acted like I was okay. I smiled and joked a lot. To them, I was the mom they always knew. The only thing different was that I had a tube sticking out of me.

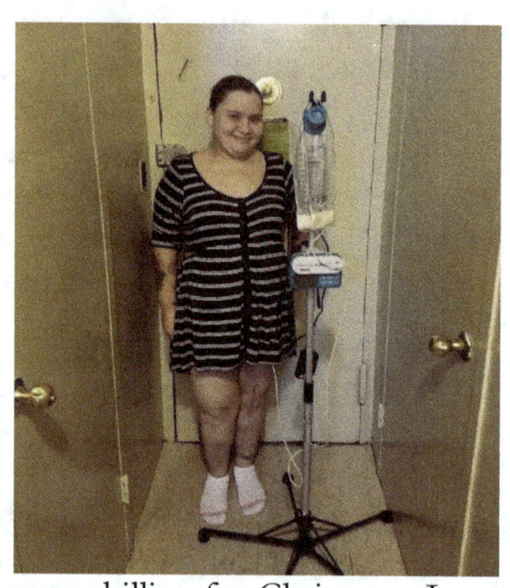

Poley and I were chilling for Christmas. I was trying to be festive and take pics.

I tried to make the best of a horrible situation. I dressed up my pole for the Christmas holiday. I drew food on and taped quotes on my bags. I didn't want to allow the experience to be only negative. I needed positivity because I was falling into a pit of dark emotions. I hated the constant trips to the ER. I hated that I couldn't really be active with my boys. I hated that I had to depend on a home attendant to help me with my daily needs. I really hit rock bottom during this time, and I felt stuck, but once you reach rock bottom, the only way to go is up. I made it my mission to grab a hold of this illness and get to a stable place in my life.

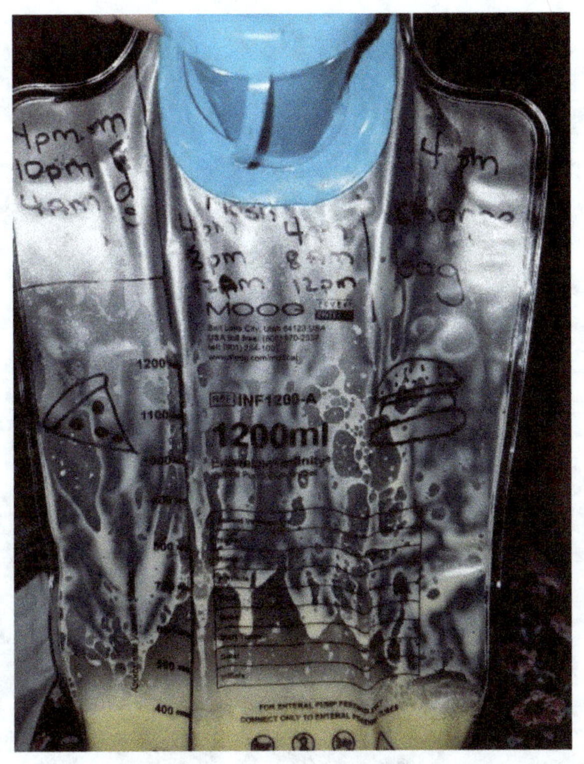

I would draw food images and write down the times I needed
to fill the bag.

This was the tubie cover that I used to control the amount of
pus that would come out of the hole.

One of the quotes I would tape to my bags to help me push through.

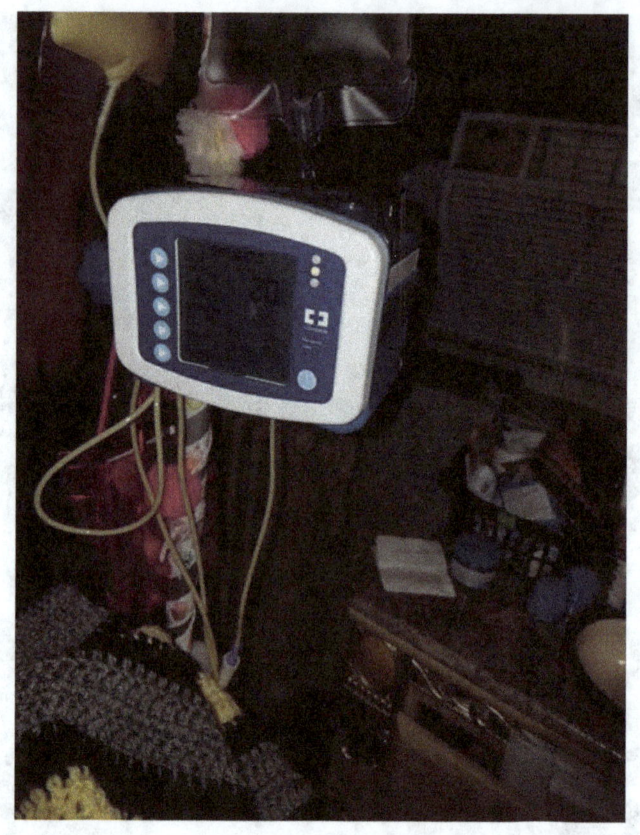

We had to figure out which rate would be tolerated by my intestine. It took me a few tries until I found something tolerable.

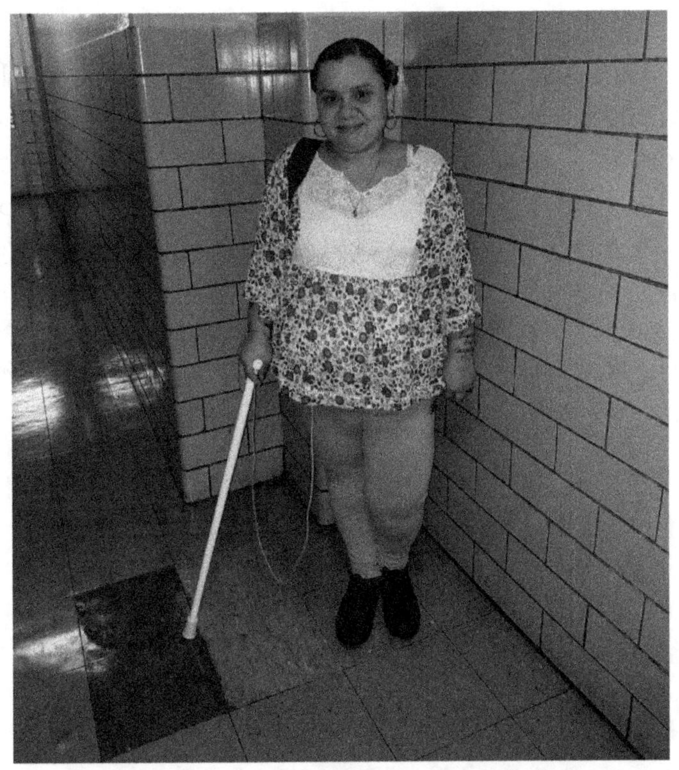

Here I am ready to go out. I have my book bag and my cane
to assist me on this trip. Smiling was one of the only ways
that I could motivate myself.

I had the feeding tube for a total of six months. At the end
of March, I had an appointment with my surgeon so that she
could perform the Gastric Bypass surgery for my
Gastroparesis. She said she had performed the surgery on one
other patient that had Gastroparesis and that it was successful.
The other patient was able to eat after the operation and she
even gained some weight. The hope was that I would do just
as well and that I would resume a normal life.

We scheduled the surgery, and the plan was to remove my J-tube, remove my gastric stimulator, perform the gastric bypass, and reroute some of my intestine due to my diverticulosis. The surgery would take up to three hours and it would be a 2-day stay in the hospital. I signed the paperwork and went about my day. I had to do all the paperwork, go to the support groups, and take all the tests that would normally take regular gastric bypass patients six months in just one month. Here goes yet another surgery and yet another new normal.

Must Haves:

- Gauze
- Surgical Tape (Look around. I had to try a few because my skin was allergic to some of them.)
- Tubie Pads (Etsy has a lot of cool designs.)
- Syringes
- Feeding tube bags
- Book bag for feeding supplies and pump
- Feeding pump
- There are other items but they're specific to the patient.

Is your feeding tube failing you?
Are you tired of being looked at as fat even though you are so ill?

Then Gastric bypass or Sleeve might be for you.

CHAPTER 8
Gastric Sleeve vs Gastric Bypass

Which surgery is right for you?

Here are some facts about both surgeries. I wish I had this knowledge when I first had the surgery. I will also add information about the gastric sleeve so that you have more options to choose from.

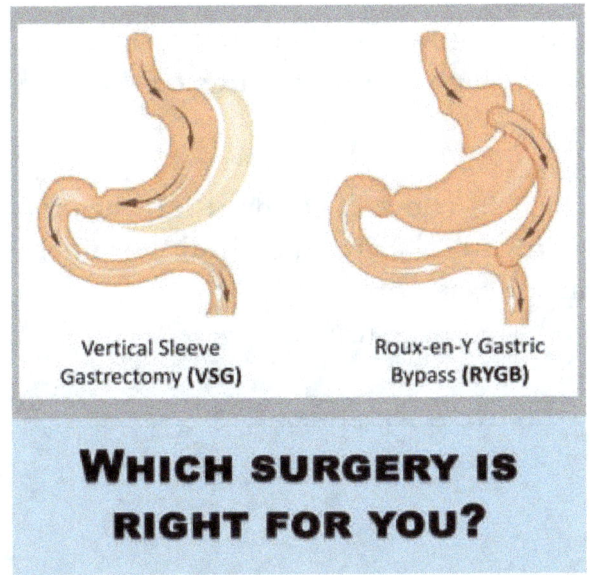

Gastric Bypass vs. Gastric Sleeve Surgery (Medicine on the Move, n.d.)

Gastric Sleeve
Known as sleeve gastrectomy or vertical sleeve gastrectomy, this weight-loss procedure is surgical. It typically involves getting to the upper abdomen by creating multiple incisions there for small instruments to get through. This procedure will remove around 80% of one's stomach.

The amount of food you are able to consume is limited because the size of your stomach is reduced. Someone who undergoes this procedure will also experience hormonal changes and these changes help the person to lose weight.

Not everyone can have this procedure done, though. These are the conditions that someone has to meet to be considered for the surgery:

- Your body mass index (BMI) is 40 or higher (extreme obesity).
- Your BMI is 35 to 39.9 (obesity), and you have a serious weight-related health problem, such as type 2 diabetes, high blood pressure, or severe sleep apnea.

<u>Why it's done</u>
It is done to help you reduce the risk of health problems that are associated with obesity. Such health problems include:
- Heart disease
- High blood pressure
- High cholesterol
- Obstructive sleep apnea
- Type 2 diabetes
- Stroke
- Cancer
- Infertility

The gastric sleeve will not help you with acid reflux. Depending on the severity of your acid reflux, this may not be the surgery for you. If you continue with the surgery, you might need a revision to the gastric bypass.

<u>Risks</u>

Although this is meant to help you, there are long terms effects associated and also short term ones that you might experience. Let's look at these below.

Risks associated with sleeve gastrectomy can include:
- Excessive bleeding
- Infection
- Adverse reactions to anesthesia
- Blood clots
- Lung or breathing problems
- Leaks from the cut edge of the stomach

Longer-term risks and complications of sleeve gastrectomy surgery can include:
- Gastrointestinal obstruction
- Hernias
- Gastroesophageal reflux
- Low blood sugar (hypoglycemia)
- Malnutrition
- Vomiting

Very rarely, complications of sleeve gastrectomy can be fatal (Reflections to Breathe, n.d.).

Gastric Bypass

With this surgery, what is affected is how your digestive system, specifically your small intestine and stomach, processes what you eat.

You stomach is literally made smaller so that you get fuller quicker, i.e. by eating less. A sort of bypassing is happening as the term suggests, which means that all of your food does not enter the stomach and small intestine. As a result, what happens is that your body no longer makes use of all the calories from what you eat(MedlinePlus, n.d.).

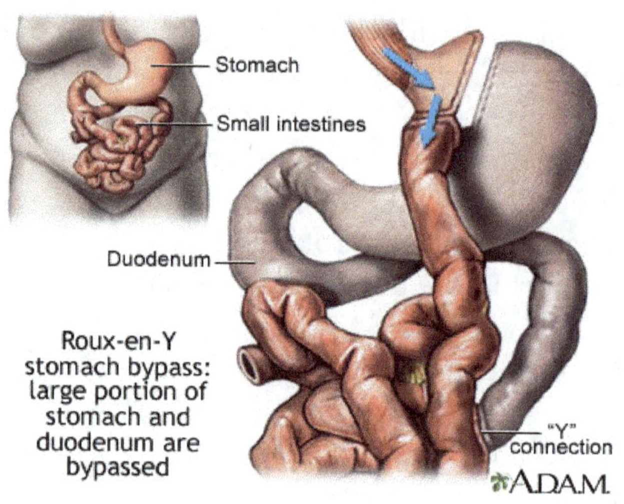

(Roux-en-Y stomach surgery for weight loss, n.d.)

This procedure may be recommended if you have:

- A BMI of 40 or more. This means that the person is carrying at least 100 lbs. (45 kilograms) of excess weight. A normal BMI is between 18.5 and 25.

- A BMI of 35 or higher, coupled with any of the medical conditions that I mentioned earlier, can often be improved with weight loss.

They will also use this surgery to help with the symptoms of Gastroparesis. It is not meant to be a cure. It is just meant to be a tool.

<u>Risks</u>

Like any major surgeries, Gastric Bypass has its risks with some of them being more serious than others. My suggestion is that before you decide to get the surgery, you discuss them with the surgeon.

Major surgeries often require the use of anesthesia—the medicine they use to reduce how sensitive you will be to pain during surgery. Here are some of the risks:

- You might be allergic to the anesthesia
- Some people get infections
- You might end up experiencing a bleeding problem such as blood clots
- One may experience breathing problems as a result
- Anesthesia can actually cause heart problems

Now, what are the risks of the gastric bypass surgery itself?
- The surgery can cause scaring inside the belly. In the long run, the scaring can cause your bowels to be blocked up.
- Because the surgery reduces the size of your stomach, if you overeat, you will likely vomit.
- The surgery involves stapling of the stomach, and as a result, there can be leaking happening from the lines in these areas.
- Stomach ulcers may develop as well as heartburn and gastritis (where the stomach becomes inflamed).
- During the surgery, you can get injured. This can happen to the intestines, stomach and even some of your other organs.
- One may experience poor nutrition.

Chapter 9

Things you Should Know about the Gastric Sleeve and the Gastric Bypass

1. The gastric bypass surgery has been the ideal weight-loss solution for many people. This is not to say that it is the solution for everyone as it has not worked for everyone. With the surgery, not all of what you eat end up in the small intestine because of the stomach being smaller and as a result, you get fuller quicker.

While we were talking about the surgery I was going to have, my surgeon let me know that my pouch would be about 3oz., 2oz. bigger than what a typical gastric bypass patient would have.

The reason for that was that I wasn't having the gastric bypass to lose weight. The goal was that I would be able to eat again. So, it was supposed to help my Gastroparesis by easing my symptoms. Basically, the food would travel straight through the pouch and directly into my intestine. The plan was that I wouldn't feel any nausea or vomiting, and I would be able to eat mini-meals a few times a day. I also wouldn't have any acid reflux. I wanted to be excited, but honestly, it all just sounded too good to be true.

2. So, who is this surgery for? I talked about this earlier but let us recap for the purpose of me explaining why I qualified. First of all, you have to be morbidly obese (and struggling to lose the weight), that means that your BMI has to be more than 35. Usually, your BMI will also be less than 49. Hence the reason you will watch programs where someone has to lose a certain amount of weight

before they can have the surgery. Essentially, if you meet the BMI requirements and your weight is affecting your daily life and ability to do things like walking around, the surgery could be the right weight-loss option for you.

I qualified for the surgery because I was suffering from diabetes, and I was also obese; my BMI was over 35. You would think that the Gastroparesis alone would do it, but no, it was the complications from the Gastroparesis that qualified me. At this point, I weighed 220 and I'm only 5'1.

If you suffer from diabetes, have a high BMI, have any other chronic health issues, and your quality of life is suffering, then talk to your doctor and see what he/she recommends.

3. It is important that you are realistic when it comes to gastric bypass surgery. There is no guarantee of you being healthy forever and it will not automatically make you fit. Remember that fitness and being the right weight are not synonymous. Once you have had the surgery, you have to do what it takes to remain healthy and fit which usually involves eating healthy, taking vitamins, and at least engaging in light exercise.

The gastric bypass is NOT a quick fix. You must remember that you will always have Gastroparesis. This surgery is just to help you manage the symptoms and help you have a better quality of life.

I set myself up for failure because I had this mindset. I thought I was going to be able to eat and live a normal life. Unfortunately, that didn't happen, and I was miserable for the first year after the surgery. So please, if you are considering this surgery, keep in mind that you still have to do the work and that this will not be the magic cure you think it is.

4. There are risks as I pointed out earlier, however, I will mention some more here. One may experience the dangers of mineral and vitamin deficiency. Some people after having the surgery develop food intolerance, others experience stomach ulcers that bleed, gallstones, low blood sugar, and dehydration. One of the things that you must do once you have had the surgery is to take vitamins. This is nonnegotiable.

Here are some of the things I suffered from after gastric bypass:

- Ulcers
- Small Hiatal Hernia
- Still not being able to eat solids
- Acid reflux

About a month after surgery, I started feeling very sharp pains in my lower chest area. It literally took my breath away; it was so painful. And it only happened after I ate or drank something. I ended up in the ER and they found an ulcer on the incision itself. They also found a small hiatal hernia. That's when your stomach is coming up through your esophagus. Mine was small, so it didn't need to be removed. I still have to eat most of my food in liquid or puree form and I can't eat a lot. They also found inflammation in my esophagus recently and they said it's acid reflux. Gastric bypass patients are not really known to have acid reflux after the surgery.

5. I already mentioned some of the complications of the surgery like stomach ulcers and bleeding problems. However, it is important to note that some of the complications can be life threatening. This is not to scare you off, but it is important that we all understand this as best as possible. A blood clot for example could be life

threatening just as much as a heart attack, which are the risks involved. Remember also that these risks are not guaranteed. Not everyone who does the surgery will experience complications and some may only experience the less severe ones like problems with digestion and dumping syndrome.

The two complications I ran into and still have today are:

- Dumping syndrome

- Digestive issues

Dumping syndrome is when your body rejects something you ate that had high amounts of fat or sugar. It can also happen if you ate too much. Due to the Gastroparesis, food takes much longer to digest, so I'm left uncomfortable for hours even if I only eat two spoons of food. I also suffer from constipation and have to take home remedies to go to the bathroom.

CHAPTER 10
Journey to Feeling Better

On May 1, 2017, I was wheeled into the operating room for what was hopefully my last surgery for Gastroparesis. I was told that if this surgery didn't work, the only thing left would be to have my stomach removed. I was optimistic that this was going to work. I refused to have my stomach taken out. I was 211 lbs. the day of surgery, and I was told that I would lose about 70 lbs. the first year after surgery.

The surgery lasted three hours and she was able to do everything she planned except to take out my stimulator. There was too much scar tissue surrounding the machine, so she couldn't remove it. I would have to remove it at another time. I was in the hospital for three days because I had some problems holding down liquids. After surgery, you are placed on a liquid diet for two weeks until you see the doctor and he can advance you to pureed foods. Some doctors start you on pureed food, but it's very rare. You must stay in the hospital until you are able to hold down a certain amount of liquids and you have a bowel movement.

The first year after surgery was the hardest time I have ever had. The mental part was the hardest. Knowing that I would never be able to enjoy foods that I once loved, knowing that I would be restricted in the foods I could eat, and worst of all, knowing I had to do this while still living up to my roles as a wife and mother, I started resenting everyone and everything. I started to become bitter, and I regretted having the surgery. I had complications from both the surgery and my Gastroparesis. I wasn't handling it well at all. I was so scared, but more than anything, I felt completely alone. I had to go through liquids, then purees and then I was supposed to start solids. I couldn't start solids at all until I made the year mark. I always threw up the solids.

I wish I would have educated myself more on the surgery and the first few months after surgery. I wasn't prepared for the mental battle I went through after this surgery. I was just willing to go through whatever I had to go through to be here for my family.

Two things I learned about the treatments for this illness were that 1) there wasn't much information or treatments out there for GP and 2) we are considered guinea pigs for the only treatments that are available to us. I think that not enough people speak out about the good and bad of GP. The main reason for this is because of how we are looked at and treated. Doctors are not empathetic to our situation when addressing our concerns with this illness. They treat us like liars and drug addicts. When they ask us what our symptoms are and we tell them, they tell us that we are not telling the truth. Yet they treat us like experiments when they want to try their recommended treatments.

Trying to smile and stay positive during the hospital stay.

This was pureed hospital food shaped to look like the real thing. It was gross and disgusting.

I started feeling better in about 2018, that was until the rashes started from the loose skin.

I now want to talk about a topic that many hate talking about including myself. It is something that happens after losing a lot of weight rapidly. It has affected me for so long and here it is: LOOSE SKIN…

It is a topic people don't like talking about because it's gross. After losing all the weight, I was left with an apron from the skin, so now it sits over my legs. The lack of air causes moisture to get trapped and without air to dry it up, it breeds bacteria and the rash starts. Here is what a lot of the rashes and cuts look like:

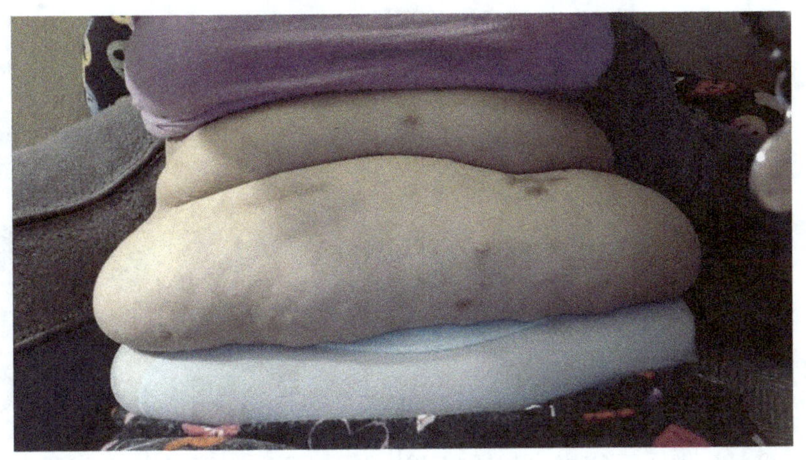

Here I am at 168 lbs. but you wouldn't know it because this is all that's seen.

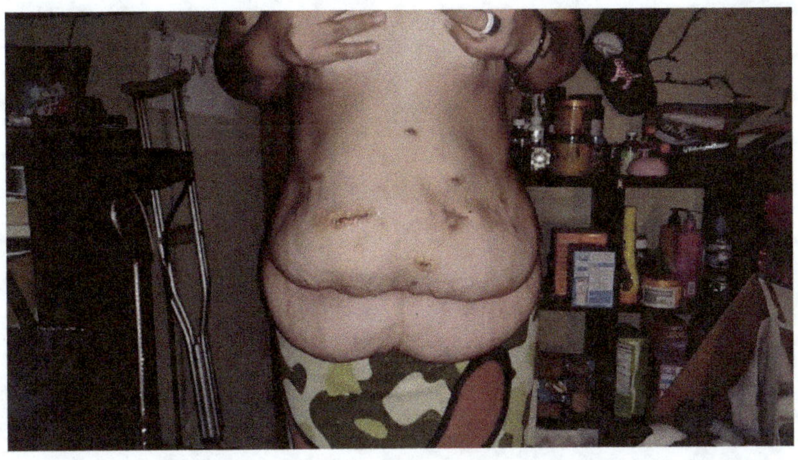

This is what my stomach looked like after they removed my Gastric Stimulator. (2019)

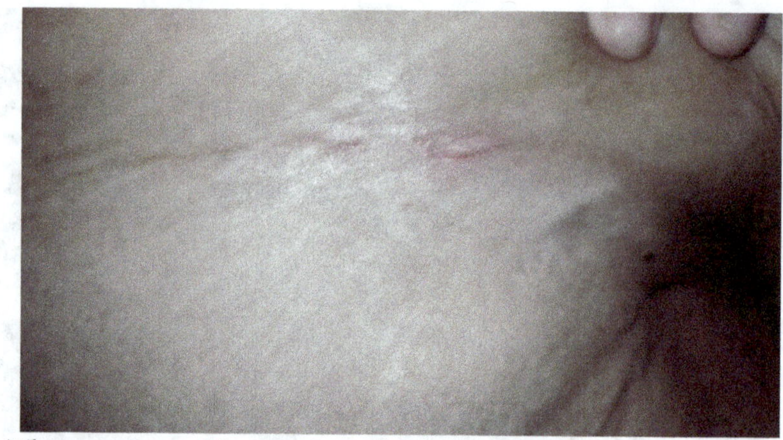

The cuts would start small and spread out because my stomach hung very low at the bottom. As they healed, it would smell really bad. (2019)

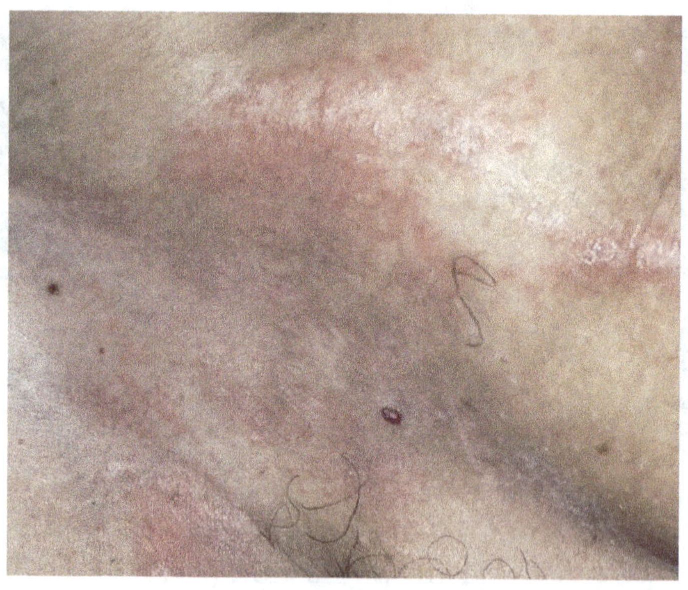

Right side of my belly area. This was right underneath the flap of skin that hung over. It itched and smelled so bad. I had to start using medications to handle the itch. (2021)

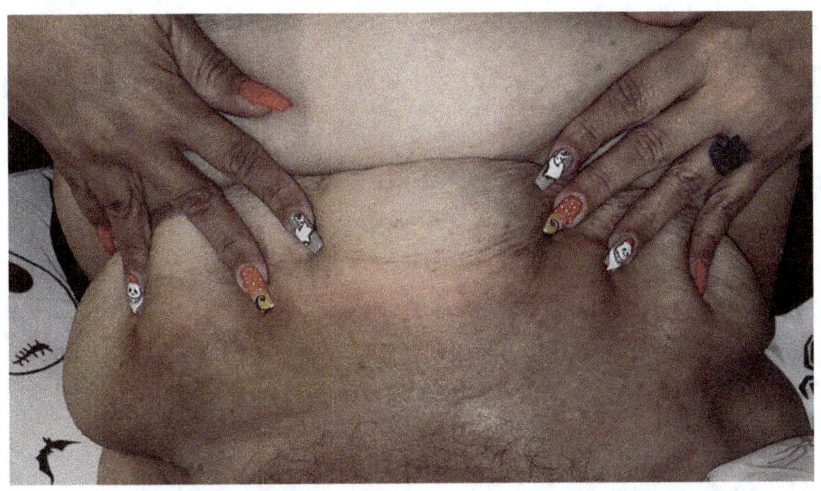

This was the worst the rash ever got. I have had many different types of topical creams and ointments that have helped with these types of rashes.

However, I am sitting here telling you that it definitely gets better, and I am living proof that this surgery can work to give you a better quality of life, if done properly and you follow the treatment plan for the rest of your life. It is not a cure nor is it a magic pill that will have you eating like a normal, healthy person. What it has given me is more time with my family. I realized I don't really need a lot of food daily to nourish my body, and most of all, this surgery definitely saved my life. Without it, I would have been a miserable person and I would have died eventually from malnourishment. Instead, I took a risk, and I'm here to tell you where my life is and where it is heading.

CHAPTER 12
Where am I now?

It has been almost five years since my surgery. It is now April 10, 2022, and I am just finishing this book. I am currently sitting at 175 lbs. and even though I am still having problems with my Gastroparesis, it is nowhere near as bad as before my surgery. I have very few flare-ups, I have been able to maintain the weight loss, my diabetes has been managed for the last four years, and my A1C is 5.7.

Let me take you back to what I gained in the last four years. I don't talk to my oldest due to personal issues he and I have. My other boys both graduated. One graduated high school and became a dad. He now streams and is a wonderful father. The other became a junior in high school, then graduated and he is now in college. I also met my beautiful daughter-in-law , whom I call my daughter and she gave me a beautiful granddaughter.

My youngest graduating.

My middle son at his graduation party.

Leamcy (my daughter-in-law) and I for her 18th birthday.

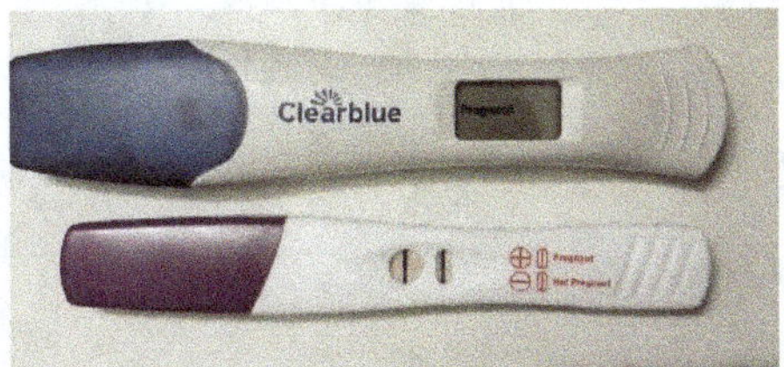

Leamcy got pregnant at 20 and birthed a beautiful little girl
(12-13-2020).

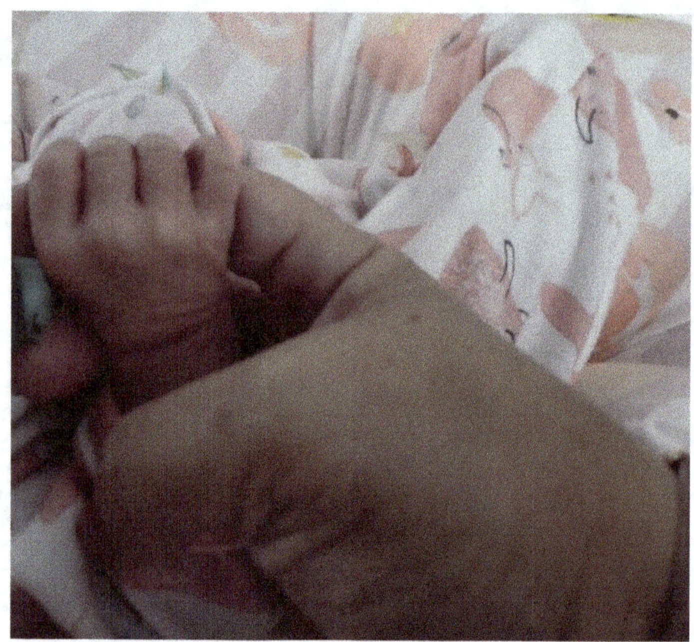

Cj and Grandma against the world.

I have also started a few businesses, one being a pet bakery. I am enjoying myself so much with it and the ideas I'm getting for it.

I am also divorced and healing myself from the inside out. My Gastroparesis is better and as long as I live stress free, my symptoms stay dormant and don't bother me too much.

At my lowest weight of 153lbs.

Currently weighing in at 175lbs. and loving life.

I finally see the light in my eyes.

Things to Remember on this Journey

The most important thing to remember is that THIS IS YOUR JOURNEY, and no one can tell you how to go through it. I want this book to just be a tool to use if you have questions, not something that is set in stone for you. These, of course, are my experiences and yours might be different, however, I hope through my story, you can decide what path you want to take.

Websites and groups I went to get help and resources from:
1. https://rarediseases.org/
2. https://www.mayoclinic.org/diseases-conditions/gastroparesis/symptoms-causes/syc-20355787
3. https://www.facebook.com/groups/chronicillnessfightersupportgroup/

REFERENCES

1. Demarco, C. (2018). *Should you get a central line for chemotherapy?* https://www.mdanderson.org/cancerwise/should-you-get-a-central-line-for-chemotherapy-.h00-159224934.html

2. Elli, R., (2012). *What You Need to Know Before Roux-en-Y Gastric Bypass Surgery.* https://mexicobariatriccenter.com/roux-en-y-gastric-bypass-facts-you-should-know/

3. Holland, K., (2020). *Nasogastric Intubation and Feeding.* https://www.healthline.com/health/nasogastric-intubation-and-feeding

4. Mayo Clinic (n.d.). *Capsule Endoscopy.* https://www.mayoclinic.org/tests-procedures/capsule-endoscopy/about/pac-20393366

5. Medline Plus (n.d.). *Jejunostomy feeding tube.* https://medlineplus.gov/ency/patientinstructions/000181.htm

6. Metheny, N. and Meert, K. (2008). *Where's the Feeding Tube?* https://psnet.ahrq.gov/web-mm/wheres-feeding-tube

7. Nashville Weight loss Solution (n.d.). *Gastric Bypass vs. Gastric Sleeve Surgery: Which weight loss procedure is right for you?* https://www.nashvilleweightloss.com/single-post/2019/07/09/gastric-bypass-vs-gastric-sleeve-surgery-which-weight-loss-procedure-is-right-for-you

8. NORD (n.d.). *Synonyms Of Gastroparesis.* https://rarediseases.org/rare-diseases/gastroparesis/

9. Oxford Medical Education (n.d.). *Nasogastric (NG) Tube Placement.* https://oxfordmedicaleducation.com/clinical-skills/procedures/nasogastric-ng-tube/

10. Whitlock, J. (2022). *Types of Feeding Tubes and Their Uses.* https://www.verywellhealth.com/what-you-should-know-about-feeding-tubes-4152086

www.ingramcontent.com/pod-product-compliance
Lightning Source LLC
Chambersburg PA
CBHW061338140726
47997CB00003B/1011

STEPPING OUT WITH PURPOSE

The Five-Pillar Path from Stuck to Unstoppable

Dr. Valarie Harris

Dedication

To every woman who has spent years being the answer for everyone else and forgot to become the answer to her own calling.

This book is the conversation I wish someone had with me sooner ~ gently, clearly, and in time for me to stop circling what God had already placed inside me.

You are carrying something the world still needs.

To my mother, whose life preached purpose long before I had language for it. I learned what faithfulness looked like by watching you show up with dignity, consistency, and love when no one was applauding. Your life taught me that purpose is not something you announce first. It is something you live.

And to the twenty-five-year-old version of me standing in Newport News with big dreams and a faith bigger than her fear: keep walking. God was not teasing you with that vision; He was preparing you for it.

Acknowledgements

This book began in prayer before it ever became a manuscript. I give honor to God, who kept pressing this message into my spirit until I had the courage to put it on the page.

To my family: thank you for your love, your patience, and your steady belief in what God placed inside me. You gave this vision room to breathe.

To the women who have trusted me with their stories through workshops, coaching, classrooms, conversations, and the EmpowerHer Summit: this book exists because your courage kept confirming that this message mattered.

To my team, mentors, and champions: thank you for helping me build with excellence, integrity, and heart.

And to the woman holding this book: thank you for trusting me with your next season. I do not take that lightly.

STEPPING OUT WITH PURPOSE

The Five-Pillar Path from Stuck to Unstoppable

Table of Contents

The Day I Stopped Circling

What are you actually called to build?

Not support. Not admire. Not postpone. Build. I want you to sit with that question before you read a single word further. That question has been living in you longer than you are willing to admit. You have felt it in quiet moments you quickly filled with noise. You have sensed it pressing against the edges of the life you have been managing so responsibly. The distance between where you are and where God is calling you is not because you lack information. It is because you have not answered the call. And this book was written for any woman who is finally ready to stop circling and give an honest answer.

You did not pick up this book by accident. Something in you recognized that it was time... time to stop explaining the delay, to stop dressing the hesitation in the language of wisdom, and finally answer what God has been asking.

I found my answer on an ordinary morning. Not a dramatic one. No spotlight. No thunderclap. No sudden burst of certainty that made everything easy. It was around six o'clock. I was sitting in my den, in my favorite chair, with a small lamp beside me and a cup of tea in my hand. My journal was open to blank pages because I had come there to pray, to listen, and to write. But that morning, I was carrying a restlessness I could not explain. A strange feeling of being tired and unable to be still at the same time. And then the question rose in me with more force than I wanted to admit: *What am I actually called to build?* I knew enough Scripture to recognize when God is pressing on something. Jeremiah 29:11 had always reminded me that God is intentional about purpose and future. James 1:5 had taught me to ask for wisdom. Romans 12:2 had taught me that transformation changes how you discern. But that morning, the question was not theological. It was personal. And it would not leave me alone.

For years, I had done what faithful women do. I worked hard. I served well. I earned the degrees. I carried the responsibilities. I showed up in rooms that needed excellence and gave it. From the outside, my life looked responsible, respectable, and full. But inside, something kept pressing against the life I had built. I had spent so much time helping other people reach their next season that I had not fully answered what my own next season required from me.

I knew how to support. I knew how to sustain. I knew how to contribute. But build? That word felt bigger. More exposing. More costly. And because it was bigger, I kept circling it.

I grew up in Newport News, Virginia, around strong women who taught me through the way they lived. My mother, especially, showed me what purpose looked like before I had the language for it. She gave her best without needing to be seen.

She served with dignity. She lived with faith. For a long time, I assumed that was the whole model: keep your head down, do the work, and never ask for more than what has already been assigned to you.

But eventually I had to face a hard truth. What I was calling humility had become hiding. What I was calling wisdom had become delay. What I was calling patience had become circling. Habakkuk 2:2-3 teaches that vision must be written and lived in its appointed time. My problem was not that God had failed to speak. My problem was that I had grown too comfortable carrying vision privately while postponing the obedience that would make it feasible.

The turning point was not that I suddenly became fearless; it was when I finally got honest. I admitted that underneath all my service was a deeper, unspoken question about stewardship. I asked myself: *Have I been faithful with my gifts, or have I been faithful to everyone else while neglecting the assignment God gave me?* The answer cost me something because I knew transparency with God would eventually require transparency with myself.

Once I answered that question honestly, I could not go back. I began to see that the experiences I had survived, the rooms I had led, the wounds I had healed from, and the women I had helped were not random pieces of my life. They were preparations, curriculum, credentials, and evidence. God had not been giving me fragments. He had been building a foundation.

This book is for the woman who knows what it feels like to carry more than she has yet fully claimed. Maybe you have been circling a dream for years. Maybe you have started and stopped. Maybe you know you are called, but you have not yet become consistent, confident, or courageous enough to walk all the way into it. This book was written for that moment.

The gap between knowing and walking is not usually an information problem. It is a response problem. The path moves through five places: Clarity, Courage, Confidence, Commitment, and Legacy. Each one will meet you exactly where you are. Together, they will walk you somewhere you have never been willing to go before.

This is not a book about inspiration. It is a book about formation. Not a collection of ideas to admire, but a path to walk. And it begins the moment you stop circling and step out.

You already know the answer. You have known it longer than you have been willing to say. Now it is time to build.

This book works best with a pen in your hand,

a journal nearby, and a willingness to tell yourself the truth.

PILLAR ONE:
CLARITY

CHAPTER ONE

The Signal in the Noise

Your calling has been speaking.
It is time to learn how to hear it.

Most women do not need more information to find their calling. They need less noise. When a woman tells me she feels confused, I do not assume clarity is absent. I assume three things louder have been talking over: Obligation. Expectation. Fear. Those voices can get so real that they start sounding like wisdom, maturity, and identity. But they are not the same as calling.

Obligation says you have too much on you already. Be grateful. Stay practical. Keep everybody else covered. Obligation often uses true responsibilities to make a false argument. Yes, you have people to care for. Yes, stewardship matters. But stewardship includes stewarding what God placed inside you. Responsibility was never meant to become a lifelong excuse for self-abandonment.

Expectation says this is who you have always been, so this is who you must remain. It speaks through old roles, family definitions, job titles, and the comfort of people who prefer the version of you they already understand. Expectation is powerful because it often comes wrapped in love. But love is not the same as permission to stay small. First Samuel 16:7 reminds us that God sees differently than people see. Heaven is not measuring your next step by the comfort level of the people around you.

Fear says slow down. Wait a little longer. Research a little more. Prepare a little more. Make sure the timing is perfect. Fear rarely announces itself openly. It prefers to sound strategic. It would rather call itself cautious than confess it is terrified of what happens if you finally move.

I know that voice. At one point — likely more than once — I looked at a bigger stage, an international opportunity, or a larger platform and told myself, this is not my season yet. It sounded mature. It sounded measured. It even sounded wise. But when I looked at it deeply, it was fear. I was not waiting on God. I was waiting on comfort. Wisdom without preservation gets lost, and wisdom without multiplication stays too small. Fear could no longer lead my Monday. Wisdom, obedience, and a sound mind would lead this next season.

When those three voices stay unchallenged, they do not just delay your calling. They distort your identity. You start to believe you are indecisive when you are actually overloaded. You start to believe you are unclear when you are actually crowded by noise. You start to believe you are late when you are actually standing at the edge of a decision.

So clarity work begins with subtraction. Before you ask what God is saying next, ask what has been speaking loudest in your life. Psalm 46:10 does not only call us to stillness for comfort. It calls us to stillness for recognition. Isaiah 30:21 reminds us that when we are quiet enough to silence competing voices, we can finally hear the way we are meant to walk.

The first question is this: *What obligations have I allowed to become ceilings?* Write them down honestly. Then write beside each one what it would look like to honor that responsibility without abandoning your calling. Most women discover there was never a real choice between faithfulness to others and faithfulness to purpose. The real issue was design, not destiny.

The second question is this: *Which expectations have I mistaken for identity?* If no one had an opinion about what you would do next, what would you pursue? What conversation would you start? What room would you build? What would you finally stop postponing? Get the answer on paper before expectation edits it into something more acceptable.

The third question is this: *What is my actual fear?* Not failure in general. Not rejection in general. Specific fear. Are you afraid of being seen trying? Of wasting money? Of disappointing people? Of succeeding and then having to carry what success requires? Vague fear is overwhelming. Specific fear is workable.

Clarity often feels less like a lightning strike and more like relief. A long exhale. A settled recognition. The women who move into their next season are not always the women who get a dramatic revelation. Many of them simply get quiet enough to hear what had been true for years.

Clarity is not missing. It is buried. And once you begin removing what buried it, the signal becomes easier to hear.

CLARITY PRACTICE

Name the voice that has been loudest in your life, and write one sentence of truth that answers it back.

Clarity is not a lightning bolt. It is the quiet that remains when the noise finally loses its authority.

CHAPTER TWO

Your Life Has Been Talking

*Purpose leaves fingerprints before
it ever announces itself.*

The student was not supposed to change my life that day. Yet she did. It was a Wednesday in an eleventh-grade Education for Employment class. The assignment that day was practical and ordinary: the students were learning how to write a resume for employment. The room itself was peaceful. Other students were working, papers were moving, and the day did not look unusual from the outside. But one young woman sat there with a sadness on her face that had nothing to do with the worksheet in front of her.

She was bright. That was obvious. But she was also frustrated and discouraged because she felt she had nothing to offer. When I moved closer, she admitted that she was scared to talk in front of other people. It was not a resume problem. It was a confidence problem. She was looking at her future through the lens of fear.

I sat beside her instead of standing over her. I told her I understood more than she realized. I shared that I had once wrestled with that same kind of fear myself, even in something as simple and exposed as singing in the choir. I told her that many of us experience fear at some point in our lives, but fear does not have to decide our future. Through prayer, practice, and believing what God says rather than what fear says, we can overcome more than we think.

That moment was quiet, but it was holy to me. Jeremiah 1:5 reminds us that calling begins before people ever recognize it. Esther 4:14 reminds us that purpose is tied to appointed moments. As I spoke to her, I felt something rise in me that went beyond teaching content. I was not only helping her with a class assignment. I was helping her see possibilities again.

The next day, she came back different. Her face was lighter. Her attitude was positive. She was smiling. And she thanked me for caring about her. That mattered to me more than she probably realized. As I walked away from that exchange, I felt good, not because I had fixed everything for her, but because I had watched what happens when a person realizes fear is common but not final. That conversation reminded me of my younger self, and it confirmed something in me: this is part of what I was made to do.

That classroom moment was not a one-off. Over the years, I saw the same thread appear again and again. I remember reminding one student that she was special and should never allow other people to make her feel less simply because they had more than she had. I remember speaking with one young man about the way he was presenting himself at work and warning him that if his attitude did not change, he would keep missing opportunities. I later watched his behavior shift and a better-paying job open up for him. Those moments were not random. They were fingerprints.

Those moments matter to me because they taught me something I now teach women all the time: your calling usually leaves evidence before it ever gets a title. It shows up in the moments when you are most alive and most useful at the same time.

I call those moments fingerprints. They are the places where your life keeps revealing the same contribution in different forms.

For me, one fingerprint was that classroom moment. Another was watching my mother live with purpose without needing applause. A third was the first time I stood in front of a room full of women. In that moment, it became clear: I was not just sharing information; I was helping women recognize and claim the greatness they had almost talked themselves out of.

At first glance, those moments look different. A classroom. A home. A stage. But underneath them, the objective is the same. In every one, I was helping women see what had been buried under doubt, disappointment, or invisibility.

This chapter is not about inventing a calling. It is about reading the pattern your life has already been writing. Isaiah 43:1 reminds us that God calls us by name. Proverbs 22:6 reminds us that direction matters early. Luke 24:32 reminds us that there are moments when our hearts burn within us because truth is being revealed in real time. Your life has those moments, too.

The Lived Experience Inventory begins with three moments. Not your biggest achievements. Not the moments other people celebrated most. Three moments when you felt most alive and most useful at the same time. Those moments matter because they often reveal the intersection of burden, gifting, and service.

As you work through those moments, ask these three questions:

What was I doing beneath the surface task?

Who was I serving, and what did they need from me?

What gift showed up that felt natural, even if it still required effort?

Then read across the answers and look for the thread. What contribution keeps resurfacing? What kind of person keeps appearing? What kind of shift keeps happening when you are at your best?

This is where many women get surprised. They expect a calling to sound bigger, more dramatic, or more exotic than the thing their life keeps pointing toward. But calling is often close. So close you almost dismiss it because it has been with you for so long.

Do not dismiss what is close. The fact that something has been true across multiple seasons is not evidence that it is ordinary. It may be evidence that it is foundational.

Your history is not random. It is not just baggage to carry or pain to explain. It is evidence. Read it carefully.

THE LIVED EXPERIENCE INVENTORY

Take a quiet moment to write three times in your life when you felt most alive and most useful at the same time, then read the thread running through all three. That thread is your calling.

Your life has been leaving fingerprints on your calling for years.

This chapter teaches you how to read them.

PILLAR TWO:
COURAGE

CHAPTER THREE

Fear Is Not a Stop Sign

The women who changed everything were not fearless. They were faithful.

Fear becomes powerful when it stays unnamed. Many women assume fear means stop, do not do it. They feel resistance and immediately interpret it as a warning that the dream is too big, the season is wrong, or they are not the woman for the work. But fear does not always signal danger. Often it signals importance.

You are rarely terrified of things that do not matter to you. The reason fear gets loud around your calling is that the calling has consequences. It asks something of you. It may require visibility, vulnerability, investment, change, and the surrender of excuses that have made delay feel respectable.

Women must learn to distinguish between wisdom and fear. Wisdom asks, What is the responsible way to move forward? Fear asks, How do I avoid moving at all? Wisdom may slow you down long enough to prepare. Fear keeps moving the finish line so you never have to begin.

I know what it sounds like when fear borrows the language of strategy. I have said things like, I need to build out the full framework before I pitch this to a larger stage. The truth was, I had already built the framework. That was not strategy; it was visibility fear dressed in professional clothes. I felt the same tension with the EmpowerHer Summit before it fully came to life. I kept waiting for conditions to align before I committed to a date. The timing never felt quite right. It rarely does.

There was even a moment when I almost backed out of the "yes" entirely. The yes was the decision to create the summit, a space where women could find their purpose. I could feel the pull to delay my own journey while I waited for other doors to open in my favor. I can still picture those tempting moments clearly: driving to the place, sitting in the car for a minute, trying to talk myself out of going. But what kept me with the yes was simple and weighty at the same time: I knew God had given me direction, and I did not want fear to become more authoritative in my life than His voice.

Fear also loves vague language. It says things like, I am just not ready, or, I need to be more strategic, or, I want to wait for better timing. Sometimes that is true. But when those words have been protecting the same delay for years, they are no longer discernment. They are camouflage.

The turning point comes when you make fear legible. What am I actually afraid of? Am I afraid of being seen trying? Of spending money and not getting a return? Of disappointing family? Of discovering that the bigger vision will require a bigger version of me?

When you name the fear precisely, it begins to lose its power. Not because it disappears, but because it becomes concrete enough to challenge. Psalm 56:3 says, *When I am afraid, I put my trust in You.* That verse does not deny fear. It reorders authority.

I also want to offer you a reframe that has changed many women I coach: fear is often pointing toward the place where growth, obedience, and impact are waiting. I do not mean every fearful feeling should be obeyed. I mean discomfort is not disqualification. Sometimes, the trembling happens because you are near something real.

This is especially true for women who have already built something meaningful. At that level, fear often shifts from the fear of starting to the fear of expanding. The local room is not always the one that scares you. Most times, it is the global assignment, the international stage, the larger mantle that would require you to be fully seen at full scale. I know that fear, too. From fear to fearless does not mean fear disappears; it means faith, courage, power, love, and a sound mind rise higher. Second Timothy 1:7 is not decorative language. It is marching instruction.

Courage, then, is not the absence of fear. It is the decision that the calling matters more than the fear's opinion about it. Joshua 1:9 reminds us to be strong and courageous because God goes with us. Isaiah 41:10 reminds us not to fear because we are upheld. Matthew 14 reminds us that Peter did not walk because the storm disappeared. He walked because Jesus said, Come.

You do not need to become fearless to move. You need to become honest, specific, and obedient.

THE COURAGE AUDIT

Right now, write down the next step you have been avoiding, then name the specific fear beneath it, because a named fear is no longer in charge of your life.

Fear may still be present, but it no longer gets to be in charge.
God has given me power, love, and a sound mind, and that is
how I move forward.

The Assignment Was Never Safe

Comfort is not the goal. Obedience is.

I remember the moment the invoice made the vision feel real. It was one thing to talk about my calling. It was another thing to attach money, time, and public commitment to it. At some point, I had to decide whether I believed in the assignment enough to invest when nothing was guaranteed. The investment was tied to helping others find their purpose and voice, but the real test was not the paper in front of me. The real test was whether I trusted God enough to move before I could prove the outcome.

I did not feel ready. The numbers did not create peace. The path did not become obvious. What became obvious was something else: the cycle of starting and stopping. It became more expensive than the risk of disobedience. Emotionally, I suffered because I had delayed obedience. That kind of delay has a cost. It drains peace. It breeds self-doubt. It teaches you to live beneath what you know God said.

I had done what many women do. I started when the vision felt exciting. I stalled when resistance came. I called my retreat wisdom. Then the restlessness returned, and I started again. The cycle looked responsible from the inside, but it was eroding momentum every time it repeated. Every retreat taught me I could abandon myself and still call it wisdom, and that is a dangerous habit for a woman with a real assignment.

The hidden cost of starting and stopping is deeper than lost time. You lose trust in yourself. Every restart requires you to rebuild a belief that should have been protected by continued movement.

At some point, I had to admit that I was waiting for an assignment from God to feel safe when safety had never been part of the promise. Presence was part of the promise. Fruitfulness was part of the promise. Provision in motion was part of the promise. But safety? No. Hebrews 11:1 reminds us that faith moves before the evidence arrives. Second Corinthians 5:7 reminds us that we walk by faith, not by sight.

That realization changed the question. I stopped asking, *How do I make this feel guaranteed?* I started asking, *What does obedience require from me now?*

Sometimes obedience requires investment before proof. Sometimes it requires a public step before applause. Sometimes it requires letting people misunderstand your timeline, your spending, or your ambition while you remain anchored on what God told you to do. I remember talking with my family about the cost. Time would be required. Money would be required. Attention would be required. The assignment would ask for sacrifices. The cost involved was huge. But after that conversation, I knew the cost was worth it.

I almost said no. I feared not being enough. I feared not being experienced enough. I feared what people might think if I moved before the provision was visible. Some people did think it was foolish, premature, or unnecessary. There were even relationships strained by the assignment. But after I said yes, doors opened. Opportunities happened. More importantly, my confidence grew, not confidence in myself alone, but confidence in listening to God over people and over the fear of the unknown. Matthew 14:28-29 reminds me that Peter had to step before the miracle made sense. Genesis 12 reminds me that Abram had to go before the full map was visible. Philippians 4:19 reminds me that provision often meets movement, not passivity.

I am not advocating recklessness. Preparation matters. Discernment matters. Counsel matters. But caution becomes counterfeit when it promotes comfort more than calling.

If you keep waiting until your assignment feels completely safe, you will wait forever. The bridge is often built as you walk on it.

The aim of this chapter is not to eliminate risk. It is to stop coating delay with prettier language. If the next step is unfamiliar, costly, and stretching, that does not automatically mean it is wrong. It may mean it is worthy of your faith.

So ask yourself plainly: *What has starting and stopping cost me? What woman has gone without what I carry because I kept delaying the next step? What would change if I made one irreversible move in the next forty-eight hours?*

The assignment was never designed to flatter your comfort zone. It was designed to grow your obedience.

Assignment Audit

Name one step you have been calling unsafe that is actually just unfamiliar, then write down the one irreversible move you will make in the next forty-eight hours, because obedience begins the moment the cost of delay becomes greater than the cost of the step.

PILLAR THREE: CONFIDENCE

Your Credentials Are Already Inside You

*Stop waiting for someone to hand you what
God has already built in your life.*

I was in the eighth or ninth grade when a teacher looked at me in front of my classmates and called me a moron.

The word landed hard because words from authority often do. It was not just the insult. It was the public humiliation, the confusion, the sudden question that can settle into a young girl's spirit: *What if they are right?*

I carried that word home, but my mother did not let it stay in charge. She told me, plainly and powerfully, Do not allow negative words to define who you are or what you are capable of doing.

Her words did more than comfort me. It returned authority to me. It taught me that other people's words are not revelation. They are opinions. And opinions do not get to determine destiny.

Something happened in me because of that moment. I made a decision I would not fully understand until years later: I would never use the authority of a classroom to make a student smaller. If I stood in front of people, I would use that position to call greatness forward, not crush it.

That wound became a standard. And that standard became part of my credentials.

This is what many seasoned women miss about confidence. Confidence is not performance. It is not loudness. It is not the absence of doubt. Confidence is a settled identity. It is the quiet knowing that your life has already built authority in you, even when the world has not labeled it the way you thought it would.

One of the biggest lies women tell themselves sounds so responsible: I just need one more certification. One more degree. One more program. One more official signal that I am ready. Sometimes education is necessary. I believe in preparation. But often that language is not humility. It is hesitation dressed up to sound noble. Exodus 4 shows us Moses feeling inadequate. Judges 6 shows us Gideon feeling small. In both cases, God did not wait for them to feel impressive before calling them forward.

Your life has already taught you things no classroom could have taught. The wound you survived. The people you carried. The reinvention you lived through. The rooms you held together. The women you helped breathe again. Those things matter.

I think of a fifty-eight-year-old woman who came to me. She was newly retired after decades in public education, many of them in leadership. She had led teachers, shaped students, and carried crisis after crisis with steadiness. Yet she sat in front of me feeling completely disqualified, not by education, but by herself. She had felt the pull to coach other women for years, especially women burning out in leadership, but every time she considered making it official, one sentence stopped her: *Who am I to charge for this?* I am just a principal.

In one of our early sessions, I asked her to tell me about one educator whose career she had helped save. She told me about a teacher who was ready to resign. My client had seen something in that woman that the woman could not yet see in herself. She sat with her. Spoke truth into her. Refused to let her walk away from her calling. And that teacher stayed. She eventually became a leader herself.

I let the silence sit and then told her the truth: You have been coaching for years. You do not need to learn how to do from scratch what your life has already trained you to do. You need to trust that what you already carry is worth building on. That became a turning point for her. Within months, she launched a cohort, stood at a women's conference and spoke without notes, enrolled private clients, and finally started the book she had been putting off for more than a decade. Near the end of our work, she said something that captured this entire chapter: Until today, I did not realize that my entire life had been preparing me for this room.

Your life experience is your leadership credential. Not just your education. Not just your position. Not just what is written behind your name. The real authority often comes from what you have had to live through, pray through, heal through, and rise through. Second Corinthians 3:5-6 reminds us that our sufficiency comes from God. Psalm 139:14 reminds us that God formed us with intention. Romans 8:28 reminds us that God works all things together in ways we often only understand later.

When I look at my own life, I do not only see degrees and titles. I see a young girl who learned not to let careless words define her. I see an educator who is committed to creating rooms where people feel safe enough to grow. I see a woman who knows what it costs to delay a calling and what it takes to finally step into it. That is credential.

This is why I want you to write a Lived Credential Statement. Not a resume. Not a bio. A statement of what your life has made you qualified to do. The question is not merely what have you studied. The question is, *What have you survived, served through, learned, and built that now gives you authority to help someone else?*

When you answer that truthfully, something settles. You stop waiting for permission to believe what your life has already proven.

You are not empty. You are not unofficial. You are not disqualified because your authority was built in hard places instead of neat ones.

LIVED CREDENTIAL STATEMENT

Write one sentence that completes this truth:

My life has already qualified me to

____

____

____

____

____

____

____

____

____

____

And let that sentence be the last thing you argue with before you turn this page.

Chapter Six

Stop Waiting for Permission

Nobody is coming to hand you the microphone.
Build the stage.

For a long time, I was waiting for the right room to notice me. I would not have said it that way then, but that is what I was doing. I was serving, showing up, leading well, and hoping that someone with enough authority would eventually extend the invitation that confirmed I was ready.

The invitation never came.

At first, that truth could have felt disappointing. Instead, it became liberating. Because once I realized that the room I was waiting for was never going to be handed to me, I understood something essential: some rooms are not invitations to receive; they are assignments to build.

I can trace one of the clearest public shifts to January 2024. That was the season when sponsor outreach began, and the first public flyer for the summit went out. Hitting publish did not feel triumphant at first. It felt nervous and weary. I worried people might think I was begging. I worried the public step would expose the size of the dream before I had enough visible proof to defend it. And when no one responded right away, I had to sit in that silence without pulling the flyer back down. That is public courage, not the absence of nerves, but the decision to stay visible anyway.

That realization changed how I moved. I stopped waiting to be chosen for a platform someone else designed, and I started building spaces for the women I was called to serve. That shift eventually became the EmpowerHer Summit. A room built with intention, ownership, and vision. Not a borrowed room. Matthew 5:14-16 reminds us that light is meant to be seen. Esther 4:16 reminds us that some public steps must be taken before they feel fully safe. Isaiah 6:8 reminds us that availability matters as much as ability.

Many women struggle here because permission-seeking has been trained into them. We were taught to contribute, not necessarily to create. To support vision, not always to carry one publicly. To make the room better, not to build the room ourselves. So when it is finally time to lead visibly, hesitation feels like humility even when it is actually fear.

There is also an approval hunger that hides underneath the habit. Support is safer than authorship. Helping is safer than being seen wanting something significant for yourself. But hiding is not humility. Hiding is deprivation, for you and for the women who need the room only you can build.

This is the shift from audience mindset to stage mindset. The audience mindset asks, *Will they notice me? Will they approve? Do I belong here?* The stage mindset asks, *What was I sent to deliver, and who needs it?* One mindset waits for affirmation; the other moves with the assignment.

I have watched that same truth show up in the lives of women I serve. One young woman came to me at a point where she was seriously considering giving up on her educational journey. She wanted the degree, but discouragement and the weight of life had convinced her that quitting might be wiser than continuing. Over twelve weeks, we rebuilt confidence, reconnected her to purpose, and challenged the lie that this was the time to stop. She did not just go back. She stayed. She finished. She earned her master's degree. Public courage is the moment private faith becomes visible.

Owning the room does not mean becoming loud, self-important, or performative. It means entering spaces with a defined purpose. It means refusing to spend your best energy wondering if you are allowed to be there. It means showing up as a woman who has already answered the question of belonging before she walks through the door.

There are three permissions most women need to grant themselves. First: permission to take up space. Your presence is not an intrusion when God sends you. Second: permission to build the room. If the platform does not exist, create it. Third: permission to be seen. The women you serve cannot be helped by the version of you that stays hidden to remain comfortable.

This chapter is about public confidence. Not just knowing who you are, but acting like you know who you are before everyone else catches up. Mark 2 teaches that sometimes you have to make a way into the room. Luke 8 reminds us that no longer hiding can become part of a healing testimony.

When the invitation does not come, that does not always mean the door is closed. Sometimes it means you are holding the blueprint.

PUBLIC STEP

Name the room only you can build. Then tell one real person what you are building this week, without apology, without minimization, and without waiting for their applause to make it real.

____

____

____

____

____

____

____

____

____

PILLAR FOUR: COMMITMENT

Purpose Is a Daily Decision

Motivation is a feeling. Commitment is a structure.

There was a season when nobody was watching. No large audience. No clear momentum. No visible evidence that the work was growing the way I hoped it would. Just five o'clock mornings in my special corner in the den, soft worship music in the background, my Bible open, my journal nearby, and prayer rising before the rest of the day laid claim to me. It was me and Jesus. That hidden routine became one of the holiest workshops of my life.

That season taught me something motivation never could: calling cannot be sustained by inspiration alone.

Motivation is a feeling. Commitment is a decision. Feelings rise and fall with results, rest, relationships, and circumstances. Commitment keeps showing up because it has already settled the deeper question: *Is this still what I am called to do?*

The private season exposes whether you are building for applause or for obedience. If you are building for applause, obscurity feels like failure. If you are building for obedience, obscurity becomes workshop space. It is where roots go deep. It is where your voice gets refined. It is where you learn whether your calling can hold without constant affirmation. Psalm 91 anchored me in that season. It reminded me that hiddenness is not the same as abandonment. It can be the place where strength is restored under the shadow of the Almighty.

I know how easy it is to confuse motivation with momentum. A woman feels inspired, starts strongly, then interprets the inevitable emotional dip as a sign that something is wrong. Often, nothing is wrong. She has simply crossed from excitement into structure.

The discouragement in that season was real. There were many tasks on my plate. Slow growth was a factor. At times, I felt unseen. There was also the uncertainty of whether everything I was carrying would come together in a timely way. Yet that is exactly why commitment matters. Galatians 6:9 does not tell us never to feel weary. It tells us not to quit. Hebrews 12:1-2 teaches endurance, not emotional perfection.

I remember one particular morning of those seasons when the weight of what I was carrying felt especially heavy. The worship music was low, something gentle and unhurried, the kind that does not demand anything from you but presence. My Bible was open to Psalm 91. I had read the same verse three times without moving past it. Outside was still dark. The house was quiet. And in that stillness, I began to pray, not the polished kind of prayer you offer in a public room, but the honest, searching kind you only find when no one else is listening.

I prayed for the children in the schools I had served. For the teachers who were burning out in silence. For the women who had sat across from me, carrying visions they did not yet trust. For my husband, my children, my grandchildren, my great-grandchildren, the faces that reminded me every morning that the work was never only about a platform. I prayed for my community, my nation, and for the people who did not yet know the God I was speaking to. And somewhere in the middle of all of that intercession, something shifted in me. The restlessness did not disappear. But it quieted enough that I could hear beneath it.

What I heard beneath it was this: your calling was never only about what you accomplish. It is about who you become in the obedience. Those mornings taught me that alignment is not a strategy. It is a surrender. And out of that surrender, focus came. Out of focus, faithfulness. Out of faithfulness, momentum, the kind that does not depend on anyone watching.

The Daily Decision Framework works in three movements. First, create an anchor, one sentence that names your calling and reminds you why the work matters. Second, identify the single most important task for that day. Not ten. One. Third, use a weekly audit so drift does not become distance.

The Purpose Alignment Audit is one of the most protective tools I know. Once a week, ask: *Am I still doing what I was called to do? Did my time this week reflect that? What is draining me that I need to release? What evidence of God's faithfulness did I see? What is my next right step?*

Commitment is sustained one step at a time, not by carrying the full weight of the whole vision every day, but by honoring what belongs to today.

Women often think the hard days are interruptions to the work. They are not. The hard days are where the work proves itself. Anyone can show up when momentum is high and the response is encouraging. Commitment is built on the ordinary Tuesday when the feeling is gone and the assignment remains.

So if you are in a private season, do not despise it. It is not proof that you are behind. It may be proof that you are being built into the kind of woman who can handle the public season when it arrives. Psalm 90:17 asks God to establish the work of our hands. Psalm 1 describes the planted life that bears fruit in season. Those verses belong to women who show up anyway.

The woman who stays is not always the woman with the most talent. She is the woman who decided the calling deserved structure.

Purpose Alignment Audit

Write one sentence that names your calling (your anchor). Then, project time in your calendar this week for the single most important task that moves it forward, because commitment is not a feeling; it is a decision you make before the excuses arrive.

____

____

____

____

____

____

____

____

____

____

CHAPTER EIGHT

Building Systems That Honor Your Calling

You do not rise to the level of your goals.
You fall to the level of your systems.

I stopped trusting willpower the week I realized my intentions and my calendar were telling two different stories.

I intended to write. I intended to think strategically. I intended to protect my best energy for my real work. But intention alone was losing to inboxes, interruptions, and everybody else's urgency. I was not failing because I lacked desire. I was failing because I had not built a structure strong enough to protect what mattered most. Systems make obedience easier than retreat. They remove the daily negotiation between your best intentions and your worst habits.

When I finally built better systems, the change was not only visible in the output. It was visible in my spirit. Before structure, I was all over the place with no steady plan. After structure, I became more focused, more assured, more grounded, and more purposeful in my thinking. Peace increased. Joy returned. Resistance lowered. I was no longer trying to rebuild direction every morning. The structure was already doing part of the work for me.

Most women think they have a discipline problem when they actually have a design problem. The evidence is simple: wherever you are most consistent, there is usually a system underneath the behavior. A schedule. A ritual. A boundary. An environment. A structure. Wherever you are inconsistent, the system is either weak or missing.

So the question is not, How do I become more heroic? The question is, *How do I build a life where my calling has first claim on my best resources?*

My business became a real example of this. Stepping Out with Purpose was born out of my own journey of faith, leadership, service, and transformation. What started as a burden in my heart had to be shaped into something tangible that could help women gain clarity, courage, confidence, and direction. I learned that vision alone is not enough. It has to be nurtured, organized, and stewarded with wisdom. Habakkuk 2:2 says to write the vision. Nehemiah teaches us that vision must also be built with structure. Proverbs 24:3-4 reminds us that a house is built by wisdom and established by understanding.

I like to frame that work through three protected commitments: creation time, restoration practice, and strategic community.

Creation time is the block of your week that belongs to the work itself: writing, building, planning, creating, thinking. It must be scheduled before less important things begin making requests.

Restoration practice is what keeps you from pouring from depletion. Prayer, Scripture, movement, silence, rest, reflection. Not as luxury, but as stewardship. For me, one of the most life-changing systems has been my early-morning time in the presence of the Lord. That rhythm does not merely calm me. It aligns me.

Strategic community is the person or circle that tells you the truth, keeps you accountable, and refuses to let you quietly drift back into smaller thinking. Callings wither in isolation.

Once those three are named, project them in three dimensions: time, energy, and attention. Time means the work is on the calendar. Energy means your best hours are not spent on your lowest-value tasks. Attention means you stop handing your first focus every morning to your phone, your inbox, or the noise of the world.

I also recommend a simple integrity check. Does my schedule reflect what I say matters? Does my environment make my work easier or harder? Do my closest patterns support my calling or slowly erode it? Honest answers to these questions can change a woman's year. First Corinthians 14:40 reminds us that some things must be done decently and in order. Luke 14:28 reminds us to count the cost before we build. Structure is not the enemy of spirituality. It is often one of its servants.

What changes when the system works is not just the output. It is emotional resistance. The work stops feeling like a constant uphill battle because the structure now carries part of the weight. The space is prepared. The time is blocked. The decision has already been made in advance.

A calling becomes sustainable not through endless self-correction, but through wise architecture. Build the structure, and the structure will carry the work even on the days when you cannot carry it yourself.

Purpose Architecture

Before this week ends, put your creation time on the calendar, name your restoration practice, identify your accountability voice, then make one structural change that puts your calling first, because a system is not a cage; it is the architecture of a life that lasts.

PILLAR FIVE: LEGACY

You Were Never Building for Now

The moment the frame shifts from personal success to generational obedience, everything changes.

There came a point in my journey when the question underneath my work changed. For a long time, consciously or not, I had been asking, *What am I building?* That is not a bad question. It matters. But it is still a question centered on me. I got my answers when I began seeing results from the work I was doing and the ways women's lives were being transformed in ways even they did not expect. I remember standing in a room and realizing that what had once been only a burden in my heart had become a real experience— women were gathering, growing, healing, and believing again. In that moment, the question shifted from *What am I building?* to *Why am I building it?*

That question changed the weight of everything. I began to understand that the calling was not mine to keep. It was mine to steward. It was not given to me so

I could build something impressive. It was given to me so I could release something useful, faithful, and multiplying.

One of the places that shift deepened in me was around missions and ministry. As I prepared to travel to Ghana, West Africa, with a team of women, I felt the anticipation and privilege of knowing I would get to minister, teach, and serve. Around that same season, I was writing my first book, Talk Time with God. The combination of those two things — writing and serving — reminded me that calling is never only about what I produce. It is about who God allows me to reach, strengthen, and send. Being a servant leader became even more important to me because I wanted God to get the glory out of whatever I did for others.

By watching my mother, I learned legacy long before I had language for it. One memory that shaped me was watching her keep going even when life was not easy. She may not have called it legacy, in those exact words, but her strength, endurance, and commitment taught me that legacy is built in the daily decisions to remain faithful, steady, and grounded. Psalm 145:4 says one generation shall praise God's works to another. Second Timothy 1:5 reminds us that faith can be carried through generations. My mother showed me that before I ever tried to define it.

This is where the frame shifts from success to significance. Success asks what I can achieve, earn, grow, and prove. Significance asks what can outlast me, who is changed by this, what am I stewarding, and who will carry this forward after me.

I have seen the proof of that shift in conversations with women. One woman later told me, *"What you said changed how I lead my family."* In our conversation, I reminded her that while her gifts were real, and her calling mattered, her life had to be built in the right order: God first, then family, then work, church, and everything else in its place. Later, she told me she could feel the difference. When she lived on her own terms, everything felt out of balance. But when she placed Christ at the center, peace, clarity, and order began to return to her home and her leadership. That is legacy proof. Sometimes one truth, spoken at the right time, changes more than a mood. It changes a pattern.

I also remember sitting with a woman who had the gift, the heart, and the vision, yet fear had convinced her to keep shrinking. I reminded her that what God placed in her was neither too small nor too late. Watching her begin to move showed me again that leadership is often unlocked by one truthful conversation. Legacy is not always loud. It is not always visible in the moment. More often, it looks like faithful presence that releases strength into the next generation.

When I began seeing my work through that lens, my decisions changed. I cared less about what made me look successful and more about what made the assignment more transferable. My questions became sharper: *Does this outlast me? Does this multiply what I carry? Does this prepare someone else? Does this reflect stewardship? Does this honor obedience even if it is not the most comfortable or immediately profitable choice?*

These are the questions of the Legacy Lens. They guide women against building only for the now. They remind us that significance is rarely measured only by what we see in the current season.

Service and obedience sit at the center of this chapter. Service keeps your work oriented toward people, not vanity. Obedience keeps your work oriented toward God, not trends. Together, they produce multiplication. They create fruit that travels farther than strategy alone can calculate. Deuteronomy 6 teaches us to pass truth on diligently. John 15:16 reminds us that fruit is meant to remain.

Legacy thinking begins the moment your questions shift from *How do I grow?* to *What must remain after me?* And once it takes hold, you do not build the same way again.

Legacy Lens

Sit with this question before you move forward: does what you are building right now outlast you, multiply what you carry, and prepare someone else to carry it, and if the honest answer is no, let that be the invitation to build differently.

The Architecture of a Life That Outlasts You

Impact without infrastructure fades.

I asked myself one day, If I could not show up tomorrow, what would continue? The answer humbled me. It came in a moment of weariness, not applause. I had spent years pouring, teaching, leading, praying, building, and showing up for others with everything God had placed inside of me. I was helping women find clarity, strengthen confidence, and step into purpose. I was creating programs, developing frameworks, leading conversations, hosting gatherings, writing, mentoring, and serving in ministry. From the outside, it looked like growth, and it was. But in a quiet moment of reflection, I realized something sobering: too much of what I had built still depended on my presence to keep it moving.

If I was in the room, things flowed. If I made the call, things happened. If I carried the vision, things moved forward. But when I paused, too much paused with me. That realization settled heavily on my heart.

In that moment, the Lord began showing me the difference between building impact and building legacy. Impact blesses people while I am there. Legacy continues blessing people when I am not. That truth changed me.

I realized I had already built more than events, sessions, and conversations. I had built wisdom. I had built frameworks. I had built messages. I had built tools that had helped women move from fear to faith, from hesitation to action, and from confusion to clarity. I had built the 7 Pillars of Transformation. I had built the W.I.S.E. Legacy Method. I had built teachings, mentorship, journals, courses, summit experiences, and leadership development principles that were not meant to stay locked inside my calendar or limited to my personal availability.

That moment clarifies that the next assignment was not just to keep pouring. It was to preserve what had already been poured. Second Timothy 2:2 gave language to it: entrust what you have received to faithful people who will be able to teach others also. Habakkuk 2:2 reminded me again to write the vision. Proverbs 13:22 widened the frame beyond one lifetime. John 15 reminded me that fruit is meant to remain.

Infrastructure is the set of structures that makes your impact continue when your availability changes. It may include documented frameworks, trained leaders, books, curriculum, repeatable systems, digital platforms, recorded teaching, assessments, automations, or a succession pathway. The form can vary. The principle does not: what lives only in you cannot outlast you for long.

I use a simple four-part lens for this work: Speak, Transform, Equip, Preserve.

Speak asks: Am I using my real voice, at full volume, with honesty and clarity? Legacy begins when you stop hiding the message.

Transform asks: Is my work changing lives, or merely encouraging people for a moment? Information is helpful. Transformation is what lasts.

Equip asks: Am I building people, or only serving them? A woman who is equipped becomes a multiplier. That is how impact extends beyond your direct reach.

Preserve asks: What wisdom is still trapped in my head that should already be living in a book, a course, a process, a resource, or a digital system? Preservation is not ego. It is stewardship. Let me say it clearly: preservation matters. The wisdom God gave you is not only for the moment you speak it. It is for the generations you may never sit in a room with. When you preserve wisdom, you make room for multiplication. When you document it, teach it, and build it into tools, courses, frameworks, and systems, you give it the power to keep working beyond your presence. That is legacy.

Technology belongs here, but in its proper place. It is not the source of your wisdom. It is a tool that can extend it. Use it to document what you know, distribute what you have built, and create access for women you may never meet. Use it with integrity. Let it amplify your voice, not replace your discernment.

When I say a life should outlast you, I do not mean it must become massive, famous, or complicated. I mean it must become transferable. Someone should be able to read it, apply it, teach it, or continue it.

Here, the five pillars converge. Clarity tells you what to build. Courage gets you moving. Confidence helps you own the assignment. Commitment builds the daily and weekly architecture. Legacy asks the final question: how will this continue?

So build a Legacy Blueprint. Name the message you are called to speak. Define the transformation your work is meant to produce. Name one person or group you are equipping. Capture what needs to be preserved before it is lost to time, distraction, or delay. Then write one paragraph describing your work as if it is already continuing beyond your daily presence.

That paragraph is not fantasy. It is direction. It is what happens when a woman stops thinking only about impact and starts thinking about architecture.

Build what blesses people now. But also build what can keep blessing them when your season changes. That is how calling becomes legacy.

LEGACY BLUEPRINT

Write one paragraph — right now, in your own words — that describes your message, the transformation it creates, who you are equipping to carry it, and what wisdom you will preserve this year; because that paragraph is not a dream, it is the first document of your legacy architecture.

What God gave me was never meant to end with me;

it was meant to be preserved with

wisdom and multiplied with purpose.

The Letter I Needed to Read

Dear Unstoppable Woman,

You are not the same woman who opened this book.

You may still have work ahead of you. You may still have questions. You may still need to practice these pillars again in another season. But something has shifted. You have named what was blurry. You have faced what was loud. You have owned what your life has built. You have chosen structure over drift. You have widened your frame from success to significance.

That matters.

As you leave these pages, do not make the mistake of waiting for another perfect emotional moment before you act. The next chapter of your life will not be built by inspiration alone. It will be built by the decisions you make when the room is quiet, the step is costly, and the assignment is still true.

So here is my charge to you:

Speak your purpose with the voice you already have.

Take the step you already know belongs to this season.

Build the room if it does not yet exist.

Protect the work with a real structure.

And preserve what God has placed in you so the women coming after you can find strength in what you built.

You do not have to become someone else to walk in your calling. You have to stop abandoning the woman you already are.

Keep walking. Keep building. Keep showing up.

The world does not need your circling. It needs your yes.

With love, faith, and unwavering belief in what you carry,

Dr. Valarie Harris

About the Author

D r. Val is the founder of Stepping Out with Purpose LLC and the visionary behind the EmpowerHer Summit, a platform she did not wait to be invited to, but built from conviction, faith, and a deep belief that the women in the room deserved a room that was built for them.

She has spent decades doing the work she writes about — in classrooms, in ministry, in coaching rooms, and on stages — helping women see what they have been carrying all along and finally giving them permission to build with it.

She grew up in Newport News, Virginia, shaped by a mother whose life preached purpose before she had language for it. She went on to build a calling at the intersection of education, faith, empowerment coaching, authorship, and leadership, not because the path was clear, but because obedience eventually became louder than fear.

Her core declaration has never changed: she is here to help women recognize the greatness inside of them, walk boldly in their God-given purpose, and build a legacy that outlives them.

If what you read in these pages has stirred something in you, do not let it settle back into silence. Take the next step, find the community, and bring the woman you are becoming into contact with women who are walking the same road.

Take Purpose Pillar Assessment: https://purpose-pillar-finder.lovable.app

Join the EmpowerHer community: www.bit.ly/4Is4chz

Contact Information: www.steppingoutwithpurpose.com

Your next season is not waiting for you to be ready.

It is waiting for you to say yes.